WHICH WAY
the
WIND BLOWS
-
A Memoir

By

JUDITH CREMER

This narrative is based on a compilation of events,
gleaned from diaries and journals
I kept at the time—
with a little help from my friends.

Some of the names have been changed
for the sake of anonymity.

The 70s now seem more like
a place to be from,
than an era to have lived.
-the author

I dedicate this book to my husband, Don,
who experienced it with me.
You're still the one!

With thanks to my "son of the right hand,"
Benjamin Cremer,
for the artwork.

"Beth Israel"— Portland, Oregon— 1976

TABLE OF CONTENTS

You never know which way the wind is going to blow,
where it's coming from, or where it's headed.
So it is with those who are born
of the Spirit of God.

-Jesus

CHAPTER ONE

WILLARD

"**O**h man! I can't believe this!" bemoaned Don. "The ice is on the *inside*!" A cloud of vapor billowed from his mouth and hung in the frigid air. He jutted his arm into the cab of the battered pick-up truck, his coat sleeve barely skimming the jagged remains of the driver's-side window. Wielding the plastic pancake turner he had rummaged out of our box of utensils, he jabbed fiercely at the frozen layer on the inside of the cracked windshield.

I was seated on the passenger side of the ancient relic, eyeing him intently, while I attempted to shelter our two children from the cold wind and tiny chips of flying ice. The engine rumbled and sputtered, straining to keep running, as we endeavored to warm the cab and clear the windows.

Our daughter, Bethany—who had recently turned two—was sitting next to me in the center of the bench seat, bundled in her stocking cap, scarf, mittens and plaid, hooded jacket. Her short corduroy-clad legs stuck out in front of her, resting intermittently on the diaper bag, as she kicked her feet excitedly and clung to my left arm. I closely cradled five-month-old baby Benjamin, thankful that the light green bunting I had crocheted for him fit perfectly now, just in time for winter.

"Here, let me do this side," I offered, taking the spatula from Don's frozen hand as he climbed into the truck. He regulated the defrost lever to its highest setting and peered skeptically at the circle clearing on the glass in front of his face. After ineffectively scraping at the ice on my side of the window, I tossed the spatula to the floor, adjusted the duffle bag at my feet and nestled the sleeping baby in my arms.

It was January 1, 1976, and it was moving day. Early that morning, we had begun leisurely loading the open, stake-bed truck, but when an icy drizzle started falling, we sped up the process. Once the damp furniture and boxes were hurriedly piled, we covered the whole assemblage with a plastic tarp, precariously bound with bits of rope and twine.

The truck was an early 1940's model, loaned to us for our move by our venerable pastor, Willard. The story held that Willard was so fond of this truck—his first vehicle—that he had hung on to it all these years, pampering it in between its use and abuse by all his church "kids."

Several years earlier, young people at Friendly Chapel—Willard's fledgling fellowship—began affectionately calling the truck "Willard," after its owner, and the name had stuck. Now all the people at our church used Willard-the-truck to move, and there was a lot of moving going on, as most of the congregation was young and transient.

"Is that it, then?" Don asked me as he cautiously let out the choke.

"Uh-huh," I nodded. Realizing my eyes wanted to tear up, I turned my gaze lingeringly over my right shoulder, and peered for the last time at our snug, little white house on Pardee Street.

Don gingerly released the clutch and the truck inched away from the curb, faltering at first, then smoothing out and gaining momentum after we turned right onto 100th. I looked back at the house and caught one final glimpse.

We stopped at busy Holgate Street and waited to make a left turn. Having relinquished the keys to our landlady the night before, we merely locked the door behind us once the house was emptied. We had already driven a car-load of items across town to our new home the previous night and, having been advised to leave the car there, Willard was brought to us and we drove him home.

Apparently, finding a parking place in our new row-house neighborhood in northwest Portland was quite a feat; once you found one, you had better think twice before vacating it, especially on a holiday weekend such as this.

We careened our load out into the traffic which, thankfully, was fairly light this New Year's Day. "Are you getting any heat?" Don wondered.

"A little," I lied. My feet were about frozen.

I tightly gripped the passenger-side window, holding it up into place with my gloved right hand. Each time we went over a bump, it fell a little deeper into the recess of the door. The wind was slapping me directly in the face, but there was nothing to do except hold the broken window in my right hand and clutch baby Benjie in my left. I snuggled his tiny face closer into my coat.

"We're staying away from the freeways," Don informed me, acknowledging that Willard struggled just to reach 35 or 40 miles per hour. When the red light at 52nd required us to stop, the old truck coughed and died. Nervously pushing a damp shock of dark brown hair from his eyes, Don restarted it and revved the engine as we swung into our right turn, then took a quick left onto Powell. Each time we turned the load we were pulling shifted, and we silently feared the worst.

By now, the sleet had warmed to a steady midday rain. As we approached the Ross Island Bridge, Don slowed down, but the truck hit a bump and then rumbled over the railroad tracks. The truck bed jolted and I caught a glimpse, in the rearview mirror, of something shiny flying off the side of the truck. I turned just in time to see one of our lamps hit the pavement, then bounce and shatter on the sidewalk.

"Your lamp fell off!" I cried.

"Which one?" His eyes darted around and for a moment he let up on the gas.

"Yours—the brass one," I answered. This Early American-style lamp was one of the few items Don had brought to our marriage. He'd had it as a boy, and it showed evidence of that with its dented base and three BB gunshot-dings on the shade.

"Well, I'm not stopping," Don decided, scarcely missing a beat. I agreed. We were on the bridge by then and that lamp was gone.

Two months earlier, on a blustery October day, I had been crossing that same bridge in a car driven by my aunt. There were six women in her station wagon, and we were encumbered with small children, babies and hot dishes. We were on our way to church that Wednesday morning for a Women's Bible Study and a potluck. A folded card table was tied to the roof of her car.

About halfway across the Ross Island Bridge, we suddenly heard a loud scraping sound as the wind tried to steal the table. My cousin's wife and I were seated by the backseat windows. We grabbed desperately at the rope, which was criss-crossed through both of the slightly-open windows and across the car's ceiling, but our attempts were in vain.

The rope and table surrendered with a horrendous screech. Startled, everyone turned quickly to look in the right and rear direction of the car, just in time to see the card table—airborne—twirling away like a giant Frisbee.

The table cleared the bridge railings and plummeted into the Willamette River, far below. For a moment no one knew what to say, whether to laugh or cry. When my aunt found her voice, she suggested we praise God because it had not crashed into the windshield of the car behind us. Typically, we all knew we could trust her to find the good in any situation. I was not as well-seasoned as she in taking that route.

We swung Willard into the right-lane and took the exit off the bridge. Now heading north along the waterfront, the downtown skyline loomed before us. This was certainly going to be a new adventure—living in an 85-year-old, nine-bedroom house in the inner city. Stranger yet was the fact that we would be living there with about fourteen other people.

We were part of an experiment our church was delving into— that of communal houses throughout the city, set up to minister to their specific neighborhoods. The houses were mostly rambling, old edifices in poorer districts, thus affordable.

Ideally, they were to be occupied by a mix of singles and families, and of both stronger and weaker Christians. The goal was to "disciple" the younger and less-mature brethren, while simultaneously ministering to the community. The commune would offer food, shelter, Bible study, spiritual support and accountability. Our youthful zeal, commitment to mission work, and the fact that Don held a steady job, made us perfect candidates for such a situation.

"I'm hungry," Bethany's tender, toddler voice broke the silence. I reached into the diaper bag and pulled out a small Tupperware container. Opening it, I handed her the snack of mixed cheerios, pretzels and raisins that I had packed. Baby Benjie was still asleep. I gazed into his sweet face, my breath causing his long eyelashes to flutter just a bit.

"I wonder who'll be there to help us unload," I ventured, attempting to make conversation. Don and I had been silent too long. We were both equally lost in thought, pondering the excitement of our new undertaking—and the fear of the unknown.

"I don't know. A few guys should be there, at least," Don answered. "They know we're coming." We barely knew anyone who lived there, and had been to the house just once—the previous Sunday—to view our rooms and meet some of the other occupants. A few we recognized from church, but we were not yet acquainted with any of them.

We had been attending the Prince of Peace Fellowship (as Friendly Chapel was now called) full-time for only five months. Prior to that, we had been involved with their coffeehouse ministry every Saturday night, for nearly a year.

The Prince of Peace Coffeehouse was popular with all the "Jesus Freaks," as tunes were pounded out on a 19th-century, upright piano with black-light overhead. When the front of the piano case was opened and lifted—revealing hammers painted in Day-Glo neon colors—the black light accentuated the psychedelic pulsation and everyone tripped out. We heard that those who wandered in while high especially enjoyed the experience.

It was there that Don was first introduced to street preaching, and soon he became one of several team-leaders who took groups downtown to witness and pass out tracts. The coffeehouse was used as the base, both to leave from and to return to, each Saturday night. Teams brought back possible converts in time to expose them to good-quality, Christian rock music and an appropriately timed altar call.

This became the pool from which we would draw people to invite back to the communal houses: those who were new Christians or at least genuinely interested, and those who were between homes or jobs and needed assistance and temporary lodging.

If we were afraid, we were disguising it fairly well. Actually, giving up all our material goods to the benefit of the Body of Christ didn't sound like such a terrifying proposal, especially when compared to what we had already experienced in our less than three years of marriage.

When Don asked me to marry him, in the fall of 1972, he had suggested two prospects: one, that we could be missionaries together and two, that we would always be poor. I had consented, for my life's goal was to be a "missionary" as well, though at the time I possessed merely an inkling of what that might mean. As for the "poor" part, I was raised humbly and I was okay with that. My parents had set a fine example for living well economically.

At 18, one's outlook and opinions are just beginning to form; I didn't yet know my own mind. What I *did* know was that I had sincerely prayed about this decision and, in my youthful hope and zeal, I believed God would coalesce Don and I together like wet clay. As we "became one" in the hands of the skillful Potter, the possibilities He could sculpt into our lives were endless.

We were both members of the Apostolic Christian Church. I was raised in it and Don had been introduced to it through a friend. We both had been baptized into the denomination earlier in 1972—I in California and he in one of their many Indiana churches.

When Don announced his plans to move to California a few months later, in order to attend college and be nearer his family, he was given my dad's phone number as a church contact when he arrived. My dad was originally from Indiana, too, and some of the people at Don's church knew him. He also was a long-time minister in the denomination, thus the reference. It seemed that Don and I were destined to meet.

And meet we did—at church, on September 20th. We became engaged five weeks later, and were married five months after that—in early 1973—shortly after Don turned 21.

At the wedding, his mom seemed visibly relieved to relinquish him into my care. Minutes before the service, she held my hands in hers and with tear-filled eyes exclaimed, "You must love Donald very much."

"Love him?" I had shrugged, perhaps too flippantly for a bride on her wedding day, "I hardly even know him!" God was the object of my love, and I was confident He would grow us up, together.

We were young and totally unprepared, but my parents liked Don and trusted him. We didn't have a dime to our name, as Don was attending college in Pasadena while working part-time for our church's elder. I was employed as a sales clerk at a Christian bookstore.

I glanced over at my husband, whose jaw was clenched and eyes were fastened on the road. We were downtown now, cautiously navigating our way through the narrow one-way streets.

One benefit to this move was that we would live less than a mile from Don's workplace. He was still employed at the same job he had found when we moved to Portland a year-and-a-half earlier. Now, instead of driving all the way across the city, he could bicycle to work or even walk if he needed to. Our country had just emerged from a gas shortage, even resorting to rationing, and we certainly didn't know what the future might hold.

"It looks like it may clear up," I offered hopefully, scanning the sky to the north and east. Portland natives, like me, endearingly called their city the Gray Lady of the Columbia due to its many overcast and rainy days.

"At least things aren't frozen anymore," was all the credit Don would give. We were almost there, but now a strong wind was whipping up.

In July, 1974, with baby Bethany in tow, we took a one-week vacation and visited Portland. I wanted Don to see where I had grown up and meet my many relatives who lived there.

During that week, we discovered the cost of living in Portland was considerably lower than it was in California. After a brief glance at the classified ads and a successful interview, Don was offered a job that paid $3.25 an hour to start. This being significantly more than his current wage of $1.95 in California, we did the math and decided to move to Portland.

An aunt and uncle of mine, who were members of the Apostolic Christian Church in Portland, generously allowed our little family to stay with them for six weeks until we were able to move into the rental house we had found, which was available on September 1st.

Don started the new job immediately, leaving me with the task of transporting our belongings, from our apartment in California, up to Portland. My aunt suggested that if I leave baby Bethany at their house, with Don, it would make my drive down and the move back up flow much easier. She offered to baby-sit while I was gone and Don was at work each day, so we agreed.

My sister, Joyce, then 14, was also visiting in Portland at the same time. It was agreed that she would accompany me on the drive back down to California in our orange Chevy Vega. Though too young to help drive, she was good for companionship—it was better than traveling alone.

Once we arrived home, my dad secured a rental trailer for me. It was a red monstrosity aptly titled "Big Bertha" in bold black and gold lettering across the side. He quickly arranged for a few days off work in order to help me drive our load north.

Upon first hearing the news of our intended move, my mother was quite upset. I didn't really understand why, but I guessed it must have hit her especially hard because she would be losing the closeness of her first grandchild. Bethany, at the age of almost seven months, was both precious and precocious, and brought so much joy to the family. Now Mom's sister and sister-in-law would enjoy the privilege of doting on Bethany, a right that should have been hers.

My dad, however, seemed a bit more supportive of our decision, although he could not for the life of him understand why I would want to return to the same city and church situation he had chosen to remove his family from eight years earlier. What he *did* understand was the wanderlust that innately permeated our family. He apparently sympathized with our conviction, if not our destination.

Nevertheless, my parents and siblings helped me pack up our meager belongings and load them into Big Bertha. But, the night before we were to leave, my dad had a vivid dream.

In it, we were about an hour north of Los Angeles, driving down the steep descent on Interstate-5 called the Grapevine, when suddenly the brakes on his car gave out. The weight of the attached trailer sent his Oldsmobile sailing maniacally down the hillside. His own screams awoke him and he bolted upright in bed, shaken and damp with sweat. In the morning, he confided his dream to us, convinced that it had been a warning from God.

In spite of that, we set out with his car pulling the trailer. But when we arrived at the 5,000-foot summit of the Grapevine, Dad turned in at a gas station to inquire if they had anything we could rent that was strong enough to haul Big Bertha to Portland.

Providentially, the station owner had just stopped by to drop off supplies and offered us the use of his own heavy-duty, extended-cab pick-up truck. He and my dad worked out the financial terms.

Confident we were heeding God's warning, we unhitched Big Bertha from the red Cutlass sedan and hooked it up to the silver pick-up. It was already blazing hot that mid-July morning in the upper desert, but we had to completely rearrange the load in the trailer, making use of the extra space afforded us by the truck bed. We then emptied my parents' car and left it parked at the gas station as collateral. They would retrieve it a few days later, on their return trip.

After a two-hour delay, we caravanned on, assured that we had thwarted our impending doom. Dad drove the big-rig and I followed in my little Vega. We rotated passengers at each rest stop.

Now, this first day of 1976, my husband and I were transporting these same household furnishings, with few additions, to yet another location. Surprisingly, my parents hadn't objected to *this* move— to the communal house. I guess they were finally accustomed to the fact that Don and I lived 1,000 miles away and made our own decisions.

What had thrown them for a loop was our decision, five months earlier, to withdraw our membership from the Apostolic Christian Church. My parents were "lifers" in this church; my dad had been elected as an unpaid, lay minister—as is their denomination's custom—before I was born.

Once our move to Portland was accomplished, in the mid-summer of 1974, the members of the small Apostolic Christian Church in Portland (the same one I had grown up in) eagerly welcomed us into their fold. They expressed their gratitude for our fresh, young vitality, and we were glad to be of use serving God in this capacity.

We found a cute little house to rent and had lived there happily these past sixteen months. Though we were staunchly committed to our involvement with the shrinking Portland ACC, it didn't take long for us to notice that God was working elsewhere.

The Prince of Peace Fellowship was housed in a century-old, Gothic structure across the river, on southwest First Avenue, famous for being the first church building in Portland to have electricity. By now the "Jesus Movement" was in full swing and most of the people attending there were our age, our generation. The Holy Spirit was moving as hippies came to know the Lord, giving up mind-altering drugs for a life-changing relationship with Jesus Christ.

Better yet, many of my cousins, and even an aunt and uncle— who had all recently left the Apostolic Christian Church—were now attending the Prince of Peace. As Don's Saturday night involvement at the Prince of Peace Coffeehouse progressed, I began attending their Wednesday morning women's meetings with my aunt.

During this time, however, our dedication to the Apostolic Christian Church never waned. We continued to attend every Sunday and mid-week service, as well as every potluck and "singing"—the ACC's social activities. But when Don offered to teach a Sunday School class, he was told they could not allow him to because he was also involved with another church (meaning the POP Coffeehouse).

Additionally, the Apostolic Christian Church maintained there was no need for public evangelism and believed that we should not call anyone a Christian who was not a member of their denomination. Because we could find no way to biblically justify these doctrines, and we didn't believe we should curtail our activities at the POP, we realized we may soon be forced to make a difficult decision.

We continued with the ACC for a full year, but an unavoidable showdown was looming in the not-too-distant future.

During the first week of August, 1975, my pregnancy with our second child was full-term, and Portland was in the throes of a sweltering heat wave. Three elders were visiting our church that Sunday for the express purpose of "excommunicating" one of my cousins, due to her choice of withdrawing her membership from the denomination.

According to Apostolic Christian Church tradition, such an action qualified one as a "heretic," causing elders to convene and make a public announcement of the infraction. Members of the congregation were all expected to stand, signifying a unanimous vote to regard the one leaving as "one who departs from us, was never truly one of us."

One elder who was present was from our former church in California. He had baptized me, performed our wedding and employed Don in his wholesale food business when we were first married.

I felt queasy with waves of contractions and nausea that morning, heavy and irritable from the heat and the bulk of my pregnancy. I also knew what they were going to do to my cousin, and it sickened me. I was disgusted by their game and knew I couldn't play it anymore. For the first time in my life, I made the deliberate decision not to go to church. Don also decided to stay home, expecting me to go into labor at any time.

After cogitating the pros and cons of our dilemma all day, and with much trepidation, we finally came to the conclusion that it was time to withdraw our membership from the Apostolic Christian Church.

That afternoon, the church would reconvene for a potluck and then have a brief intermission, followed by an evening service. We decided Don would go there alone and request a private discussion with our elder during that intermission.

He did so, but the elder insisted on including the other two visiting elders and both of the Portland church's ministers (one was my uncle, the other a cousin) in the meeting.

Don explained to them that we could not support the manner in which they had ousted my cousin, and all other members who chose to leave their church. He further expressed that we could not deny that Christ had instructed us all to evangelize. Thirdly, he contended that it was obvious there were throngs of people throughout the world who were Christians and were not members of their denomination.

Naturally, voices rose and an agreement could not be reached, as these three points are foundational to the Apostolic Christian Church belief system. This meeting blended all the elements necessary for our catalyst, for sadly, it resembled an inquisition: five ACC-steeped men, ranging from middle-aged to elderly, dourly pelting one young man with their doctrine, urging him to rescind. Don, a mere 23 years old, was cornered, naively clinging to his simplistic faith in the gospel, pitifully unable to defend himself.

Our decision to leave was momentous and emotionally charged for me, having been raised in this church from day one. Thankfully, Don viewed it more objectively, having been subject to their indoctrination for only three years.

In hindsight, I am amazed that these otherwise loving and warm-hearted people could practice such drastic measures for the protection and preservation of their sect.

Being convinced this was the right thing for us to do didn't necessarily make it easier. The hardest part was still to come—that of explaining it to my parents. Needless to say, it left them disarmed and grieving.

Our "heresy" and consequential excommunication were procedurally announced a week later, in both our former California and our current Portland Apostolic Christian Church congregations. Thankfully, we were not there to endure it; we were otherwise occupied giving birth to our son.

In the wake of all that turmoil, joining the Prince of Peace was a breeze—a living breath of fresh air. We directly phoned Pastor Willard and explained our desire. He welcomed us with a simple, "We'd love to have you. Just start coming!" What could be easier? What could be freer?

We plunged right in to what they were all about and now, less than five months later, we were "forsaking all" and moving into one of the POP communal houses. We were fearless and full of faith; it all sounded so safe. Surely Willard wouldn't steer us wrong.

CHAPTER TWO

BETH ISRAEL

By the time we made our last turn, a left onto northwest Hoyt Street, rain was falling steadily and the tarp was whipping wildly in the wind. We slowed to a stop in front of our new home— a looming, three-story house called "Beth Israel." It was wedged between a four-story apartment building and another three-story frame house that was twice the size of Beth Israel, and painted a foreboding dark brown.

There, just as we had left it, was our light green '68 Chevy Biscayne parked in front. As expected, there was no place to park, so Don put on a turn signal and left the truck idling, double parked, in the street. This must be what people do, I supposed, when they live downtown and need to load, unload or make deliveries.

Don jumped from the truck's cab and dashed through the rain to the curb, then up the stoop to the ample front porch. I watched as he knocked, opened the door and stepped shyly inside. I wondered who we would find at home, since it was New Year's Day.

In a moment, two guys joined him on the porch and peered intently through the rain at our load. A heavy-set young woman appeared at the door wearing an ankle-length, paisley-print, smock dress with a navy blue turtleneck underneath. Her long, brown hair was tied back by a dark blue bandana. Recognizing her as Sherry, I waved enthusiastically. She smiled at me and waved back.

Don motioned for me to come, but I needed help getting the sleeping baby, the bags, and Bethany out of the truck; I motioned back for him to come to me. He did so, opening my door and scooping up Benjie out of my arms. He also grabbed the duffle bag and sprinted through the rain up onto the porch.

I hoisted the diaper bag strap over my shoulder and got out of the truck. It was idling roughly, as if at any second it was going to die. I didn't care what it did now, as we were finally at our destination. Bethany scooted over towards me and I helped her down. She timidly stepped out onto the drenched pavement, then I grabbed her hand and we ran up to the house.

Stepping inside the foyer, we re-introduced ourselves to Sherry, Ted and Jay. The previous Sunday we had met Sherry, who told me that she was the "kitchen steward," but would gladly pass that responsibility on to me. We had met Jay last evening when he helped unload the stuff from our car. He had curly brown hair and a ready smile. Ted looked familiar from church—a gangly, blond guy, awkwardly shy, but helpful. Both were wearing faded, ragged jeans and plaid flannel shirts.

Don passed Benjie back to me. He had already tossed the duffle bag into the foyer and it lay at the foot of the grand, open stairway. I completely entrusted the unloading of Willard to my husband and the other capable men, and chose to not even look at the state of our things in the back of the truck. Our trip to Beth Israel seemed to have taken forever, with the rain and the reluctant, chugging engine. It felt so good to finally be out of that truck and to have arrived safe and sound.

I followed Sherry's Birkenstock-shod feet as she led us up the three-tiered staircase: three steps, a right turn and seven more steps, another right turn and four final steps, deposited us onto a spacious second-floor landing.

I already knew which rooms were to be ours; we had been given the two on the left, at the rear of the house. We had decided the bedroom on the left, with the pale blue and white floral wallpaper, was to be for our kids. The door on the right led to the bedroom for Don and I.

Immediately to my left, at the top of the stairway, was a closed door that I was told led to the third-floor attic. Next to it was a small half-bath with only a toilet and sink. An antique, oak telephone stand was against the wall directly ahead of me. The beige, rotary-dial, desk-model phone, I was told, could be shared by everyone rooming on the second and third floors. To the left of the phone stand was a full bathroom, including a large tub. A small room on the right of the stand contained only a shower. These partial baths looked as though they had once been closets. How handy, I mused, that remodeling had already been done to accommodate a community of residents here.

We walked into the kids' empty room, where I laid the baby and the diaper bag on the floor. The carpet in there was the same kind as downstairs, beige, and in fairly good condition. I pulled a blanket out of the diaper bag and placed it under Benjie, then removed his bunting. I took off Bethany's coat, hat and mittens, and hurried her into the nearest bathroom. She wasn't completely potty-trained yet, even though I had desperately tried to get her there before the baby was born. Thank goodness this time she was dry.

Sherry smiled from the doorway. "I have to get back down to the kitchen," she said. "My kids are eating lunch. Do you want me to make you something?"

"Oh, no, I brought some lunch for us. I also have groceries I brought from our house that I need to put away here. I'll be down in a minute," I replied, and then I thought, hmmm... That probably sounded too abrupt and independent. I'm going to have to become more open to people's offers of help and quit being so self-sufficient.

I removed all our wraps and, for lack of a better place, I spread them out on the floor to dry. Next, I changed the baby's diaper. He was content to lie on his back, kicking and cooing while he looked around.

I brushed out my long, damp, frizzing hair and wiped the rain splatters off my wire-rim glasses while scanning the room. It was easily big enough to hold Bethany's twin bed, Benjie's crib, the changing-table and their shared dresser. Quickly deciding where to place their furniture, I felt exhilarated at the prospect of making this house our home. I enjoyed setting up house, especially fitting things into a limited space and achieving a sense of symmetry.

There were two sets of tall, double-hung windows in the room. One set faced the dismal brown siding of the house next door, barely three feet away. The buildings were spaced just wide enough apart for a person to walk between them. The other set of windows, at the back of the house, faced north overlooking a small patch of fenced-in yard. Peering down at the winter-dried weeds that filled the enclosure, I judged it couldn't be more than a 25-foot square, surrounded on three sides by slipshod, decaying wooden fences.

Viewing the backs of the neighboring houses, I was amazed at how dilapidated they were. Immediately I fell in love with it all because, even then, I adored Victorian architecture. My excitement rose as I felt like I had been transported into a neighborhood right out of *A Tree Grows in Brooklyn.*

The yard was empty except for a discarded wooden table lying on its side with one leg missing. I pondered the possibility of putting in a garden. We had planted a big garden at our Pardee Street house the previous spring, and it had produced fairly well until August. Then when the heat spell set in and the baby was born, I finally surrendered, letting the weeds win the victory.

Little Benjie, still content with lying on the floor, was now being entertained by Bethany as he stared at the ceiling. I glanced upward too, noticing an antique, etched-glass fixture over the light bulb on the 10-foot ceiling. A roomy closet was on the interior wall. Looking in, I observed that only one thing could have made this better: if it had a connecting door into our room. Alas it didn't, but you can't have everything.

Leaving Benjie for a moment, Bethany walked with me into our room. It had dark, olive green carpet, flattened by wear, and pale yellow walls that appeared clean enough. A regal-looking, over-stuffed, red leather chair had been left in the room, in front of the window overlooking the backyard. Neat, I thought. I wondered if we would get to keep it in there.

Our room was exactly the same size as the kids', just with an opposite lay-out. The view out our side window was of the dark green wall of the four-story apartment building next-door; it had caught my attention when we arrived. There was a little more space between our house and that one—about six feet; maybe it had been just wide enough for a Model-T to fit through.

"Come on Neenee," I gently called to Bethany, as I returned to the kids' room to retrieve the baby. Carrying Benjie and holding Bethany's hand, we made our way downstairs. Our belongings were filling the foyer.

"Wow! It looks like you're almost done," I observed, as Ted blew through the front door. Peering out a latticed window, I noticed Willard was nearly emptied, but the wind was outdoing itself. Jay and Don were struggling against the gale as they maneuvered their way around the furniture and appliances on the truck bed. I had no idea how the truck was getting back to its owner, but I was sure Don would figure that out. Ted straightened up and stretched to catch his breath after plopping one of our heavy boxes of books onto the floor. He didn't answer my comment, but managed a slight grin.

Next came the hard part. Bringing in our huge Coppertone refrigerator, wood-trimmed brown couch, and washer and dryer would be a daunting task, especially up all these stairs. The stuffed, brown fabric couch had been handed down to us by Don's mom when we got married. It had a matching rocking chair that I hoped we could fit into the parlor, as I liked sitting in it to nurse the baby. It didn't look like there was room for our couch in there though, as I noted a stuffed, gray-blue velour one already in place in front of the picture window.

Bethany heard children chattering away in the kitchen, so I released her hand, allowing her to wander down the hall toward the voices. Lingering in the foyer for a moment, I noticed an interesting, old-fashioned, framed print of Jesus ascending into heaven, surrounded by angels.

Then I paused to read a poem on the wall between the stairs and the hallway. The text was written below an ink sketch of a cityscape, about one foot square, framed in antiqued-gold wood. Painted abstractly in pastel water colors, it portrayed an inner-city scene—similar to the one we now found ourselves in—with decaying century-old buildings, some with fire escapes and clothes-lines ornamenting their exteriors. The poem read:

> Though time wears the stones
> And the story grows old,
> The Shepherd of love
> Still watches His fold.
> His light still shines
> Over city and mart
> And His voice still speaks
> To the listening heart.
>
> -Unknown

A lump formed in my throat as I read the words, and I paused, allowing the emphasis of them to soak in. How awesome! I thought. This poem perfectly defines our mission here in this house!

Holding back the tears, I walked out to the kitchen, adjusting Benjie in my arms. Sherry was wiping the counter and Bethany had joined two small children at a table in the windowed nook.

"That poem by the stairs is so neat," I sighed. "Do you know whose it is?"

"What poem?" Sherry asked, absentmindedly. Distracted by running the water and wringing out a dishcloth, she didn't even turn to face me.

"The one about the city and time wearing the stones," I described.

"Oh, I don't know," she shrugged. "I never really looked at it."

Returning to the foyer, I found the infant seat and knelt to strap Benjie into it. Locating our duffle bag, I unhooked the clasp and retrieved the lunch I had packed. Don's Navy duffle bag was finally coming in handy. Last year I had almost given it away, but he stopped me in the knick of time. He had been in the Navy from 1970 to 1972, and even though his career was less than brilliant, he sentimentally valued his gear.

On my way back to the kitchen, I noticed a closet-sized half bathroom in the hallway. Its situation under the staircase gave it a sloping ceiling.

The kitchen was ample and in an updated condition, though rather stark. The tall, gaunt windows were curtainless. Peering out the windows over the sink, I studied the brown house next door. Its window was offset to ours in order to prevent occupants from looking directly in at one another, but I was positive that if they reached out their window and we reached out ours, we could shake hands.

"Wow!" I exclaimed, "A dishwasher! This will be my first time ever using one." Sherry merely smiled.

A windowed back door opened onto a small utility porch with stairs leading down to that patch of overgrown yard I had seen from above. A kitchen table and four chairs were in the well-lit nook off the kitchen, again with lean, bare windows. I sat down in the only available chair and gave Bethany her lunch.

Sherry introduced her two young children who were at the table eating peanut butter and jelly sandwiches. Her son, Justin, was six and daughter, Betsy, was four. Both had unbrushed hair and wore mischievous grins and scruffy-looking, second-hand clothes.

"I didn't even know you had kids," I said.

"They were at their dad's when you were here last weekend," she recalled. She then explained that she had been married for four years and now was divorced almost three. "This is the third communal house I've lived in," she confided, "but I think I'll move to 'Joshua House' pretty soon. It's over in northeast."

"Oh, really? Why?" I wondered.

"It's too big here, and too busy. There's always too much going on," she explained. "You'll see. Oh, I'll make dinner tonight so you don't have to, and then we can go over the menus and schedules tomorrow." I was relieved to hear that, so I got a glass of water and sat back down at the table to nurse Benjie while eating my lunch.

Man, that's a lot of moving, I thought to myself, as I silently allowed my gaze to follow Sherry around the kitchen. It made we wonder if she had a hard time getting along with the people in the houses.

I mentally tallied up at least eight, maybe ten, Prince of Peace communal houses. I took a moment to consider each of their names, for I thought they were all quite clever and unique. Most were named after a biblical person—such as "Joshua" or "Gabriel," or a spiritual attribute—like "Grace" or "Thanksgiving."

Our house, "Beth Israel," meant "House of Israel" and, in this context, we believed that Christians were the "spiritual Israel" of today. The ministry of our Beth Israel house was in all aspects similar to that of the synagogues of the Bible, in that we provided a place for studying the scripture, gathering for fellowship, and even a "hostel" offering temporary lodging to the displaced. Coincidentally, there was a Jewish synagogue in the neighborhood bearing the same name.

There was a lot of banging and thumping going on out front as the guys brought in the big furniture and heavy appliances. For the next couple of hours, Don and the brothers lugged all the things we would not be using at Beth Israel up into the attic. While tending the kids and setting up our rooms, I watched as the parade of goods was maneuvered up both multi-tiered, interior flights of stairs. This included our couch, washer and dryer, dinette set, coffee and end tables, small appliances, lamps and a myriad of boxes. Once again, I was glad I was not a man. Don was sure going to be beat by tonight.

After Don brought the crib up and put it together, I was able to put the baby down for his nap. Bethany rarely took naps anymore, and she was much too excited today for me to put forth the effort, so I let her continue playing with the other kids.

As the afternoon wore on, I continued arranging, setting up and putting things away as they were brought upstairs to me. By dinner time, everything was out of the foyer and only a few boxes remained stacked in our room.

Shortly before 5:30 we were called downstairs into the spacious dining room. A huge, rectangular wooden table, that looked handmade, was positioned with one end up against the far wall. Don and I laughed as we mentioned that our giant tapestry of *The Last Supper*, a wedding gift from a co-worker in my Christian bookstore days, would look perfect hanging above the table. Right before sitting down, Ted helped Don tack it up into place on the previously bare wall.

During dinner everyone joked about how appropriate the tapestry was, for any one of our "suppers" at Beth Israel may be our "last." Consensus had it that the food was usually skimpy and the money was always tight. Sherry served us a casserole that evening, and we met most of our other housemates around the table. At present there were 15 of us, including children.

While I ate, I scanned the dining room noticing a bay window on the wall that faced the green apartments. Heavy, beige drapes hung at the windows. There was a low table centered between the three windows of the "bay," holding a stereo with a turntable, and a stack of phonograph records.

Just off the rear of the dining room was a small bedroom we were told belonged to Jon, who wasn't home yet tonight. In an earlier era it may have been the maid's room or a butler's pantry. It was fun to imagine what life would've been like for the original owners of a home this opulent.

Dividing the dining room from the parlor was a lovely pair of pocket doors, which, when opened, slid into a recessed slot, or "pocket," in the wall. There was a large fireplace on the outer wall of the parlor, with an attractive, white-painted mantel and moldings. I was sure I could squeeze my rocking chair in there beside it. The parlor window wasn't bay-style, but it was a large, ornate picture-window with the top section crafted out of leaded-glass.

The front foyer had a matching, leaded-glass window above the telephone console. The stately front door was windowed and had a transom above it and foot-wide, latticed-glass panels on both sides. The broad front porch spanned the width of the house, with pillars and railings enclosing it. The exterior of the house was painted yellow with dark brown trim.

We learned that Beth Israel was currently owned by an order of Jesuit priests who had formerly occupied it. Now they were housed in a more modern three-story apartment building across the street. The Jesuits had lived in the house communally, reformatting it for their purposes. That explained the many separate, partial bathrooms, bedrooms in the basement, and the dormitory-style attic.

The house had a total of nine bedrooms: three in the basement, one on the main floor, four on the second floor, and then the full attic. There were two full bathrooms and three half-baths. I had been in only two of the other Prince of Peace houses, but this one seemed by far to be the biggest and the nicest.

Don and I had been assigned the title of "house heads" by Willard, when we took on this task. Don would be the "house head over spiritual matters." We correctly assumed this meant he was to lead Bible studies and solve problems. I was to be "kitchen steward," which meant I was in charge of the meal planning, the shopping, and scheduling the cooking and cleaning—as well as doing the lion's share of it myself.

Sherry was currently kitchen steward but, word had it, she wasn't a very good one and everyone—including her—agreed she should be relieved of her duties. I felt certain I was up to the task because I was efficient and well organized. My confidence was shaken a bit, however, after I discovered that, at a mere 21 years old, I was the *youngest* sister in the house. I wondered if, in order to better carry out my authority, I should try to keep my age a secret.

Sundays were "free day" as far as the kitchen was concerned, which meant I was responsible to provide a breakfast plan but no other meals. That gave everyone the opportunity to spend the day with friends, family, or to eat out. Most of the singles had parents in town, and they visited them on Sundays after church. This seemed odd to us at first, since we were now accustomed to living far away from family.

As these things were being explained, it dawned on us that we were presently the only married couple in the house.

Four of the Beth Israel guys worked at Noah's Ark Leatherworks, several blocks away, on 21st and Lovejoy. It was a leather shop by day, where they fashioned top-quality wallets, belts, key fobs and Bible covers. On Saturday nights, it was transformed into a coffee-house, similar in style to the Prince of Peace, though much smaller.

The Prince of Peace Coffeehouse could hold a couple hundred people, while Noah's Ark would have trouble containing 50. It was a quaint, hole-in-the-wall storefront, near a busy intersection. Noah's Ark was a specific ministry of the Beth Israel house, and we house members were committed to manning it every Saturday night. Don switched his allegiance to the Noah's Ark Coffeehouse, and used it as his base for street-witnessing upon our move to Beth Israel, though he preferred the intensity and excitement of the POP Coffeehouse. He hoped he could return there at least one Saturday night a month.

In addition to our rooms, the second floor held two other bedrooms, which faced the front of the house. Sherry and her children occupied one, and two single girls, Ann and Terry, shared the other. Ann, a sweet, diminutive blond, was a kindergarten teacher at a Christian school. Terry, an outgoing brunette, was a sales clerk at Meier and Frank's department store downtown. Sherry didn't have a job, so I assumed she received alimony, child support or welfare.

The attic dorm, directly above our rooms, currently housed two single guys. The front half of the attic held everyone's stored goods. It was weird knowing that we were all into this scene temporarily, yet no one knew for how long. It felt to me like our lives were on hold.

We were told that Jon, who was "house head of finances," collected the rent every Friday. It cost $40 a week for each adult and $10 per child to live at Beth Israel; babies were free. This fee was to include our housing, all utilities, groceries and household supplies. After dinner, we handed Jon $90 to cover our little family for our first week.

In their wisdom, before our arrival, the Prince of Peace leadership had determined that the needs of each communal household could be met by a weekly allotment of $5 per adult and $2 per child, for food and household supplies.

After receiving everyone's rent, Jon would dole out the grocery money to the kitchen steward. Consequently, after we paid him, he tallied the allotment and handed me $66. I would begin my "job" Monday morning and was expected to feed 12 adults and three children with this money for the coming week.

Upon paying their rent, everyone was allowed to keep the remainder of their own money, spending or saving it however they chose. We liked this system and believed we could actually get ahead, for it was cheaper than living privately.

The house already had a washer and dryer in the basement, so we stored ours up in the attic. Rather than lug our monstrous freezer-on-the-bottom refrigerator up all those stairs, we decided to plug it into a corner of the dining room, optimistically thinking it might be needed for grocery overflow.

We placed our bookshelf unit and the majority of our books in the parlor to share with the house. Most of my kitchen appliances and cookware fit, and were needed, in the house kitchen. We decided to hang several of our pictures and plaques on walls throughout the house, making it feel more like home to us. When I hung my *Kitchen Prayer* plaque over the stove, Sherry commented dryly, "This kitchen needs prayer."

She was a little different, I thought, but I'll get used to her and we'll get along okay. I had never known any single mothers before; I had only been around Apostolic Christians for 20 years. I could adjust.

The Cremers pause on the stoop at Beth Israel before heading to church one Sunday morning in January.

CHAPTER THREE

MIRACLES

When the alarm clock's rude blaring shattered the stillness at 6 a.m., I struggled to open my eyes, surveying the smoky grayness of our room. Don climbed over me, shuffled out of bed and crossed the room to silence the sound. We had placed the clock on the desk at the foot of our bed, so we would purposely have to get up to turn the annoying thing off. I closed my eyes and snuggled back under the covers, thankful that I got to stay in bed a tad longer. I had just been up between 4:30 and 5 changing and nursing the baby.

Now at 6, it was Don's turn to begin his daily regimen by bringing in wood and building a fire in the parlor fireplace. He dressed quickly, and quietly closed the door behind himself, leaving me in our chilly room. I groggily recalled the house rule requiring the thermostat to be set under 60 degrees at night. I hoped that when Don got to the bottom of the stairs he'd remember to turn it up to 65, the maximum allowed during the day. Our country was in the throes of an energy crisis, so our frugality was based on allegiance to this cause, as well as financial necessity.

I dozed until 6:25, then dragged myself out of bed and into the bathroom. It was Monday morning—our first weekday in the house—and time for our first mandatory, morning house prayer meeting. I wasn't sure if I should get dressed or merely wear a bathrobe over my nightgown. I opted for the bathrobe, then peeked in the kids' room to see if they were still asleep. So far, so good, I thought, and tiptoed down the stairs.

The hearth was ablaze with light and warmth as I entered the parlor. Don was seated on the floor in front of the fire, still wearing his Navy pea coat over his sweats. Jon was near him, sitting cross-legged, tuning his guitar. He reminded me of Art Garfunkel with the addition of a full beard and wire-rimmed "granny glasses" like John Lennon's.

Jay was in a knee-length, weathered red-and-beige-striped, velour bathrobe, paired with unlaced muddy hiking boots. I figured he must have been the other brother on "firewood duty" with Don.

There was a list posted on the refrigerator detailing everyone's chores, on a rotation system. The brothers took turns, in pairs, chopping wood and stacking it on the porch each evening, and then bringing it in the house and building the fire at 6 each morning. Brothers were also responsible for emptying the garbage daily. Sisters took turns preparing breakfast each morning during the prayer meeting. The table had to be set and food ready to serve when the pocket doors slid open at 7 and everyone filed into the dining room.

I sat in my rocker by the fireplace, with Don at my feet. In the next couple of minutes the room filled up, and I realized that my bathrobe would do. All the other guys were dressed, but the women were still in bathrobes. Terry was making breakfast today; I would have my first turn tomorrow.

Jon began playing the guitar and led us in a few scripture songs, familiar to us all from church. Jay accompanied him by keeping rhythm on a tambourine. We sang directly from our King James Bibles—Psalm 108, "Awake psaltery and harp; I myself will awake early,"—as the fire snapped and crackled merrily, and the parlor grew lighter with the morning sun.

After several choruses, prayer began with one person leading. Everyone then took their turn around the circle—each expressing prayer for both house and personal needs—while the others all agreed, "Yes, Lord," "Amen," or subtly whispered in unknown tongues of the Spirit.

Jon wrapped it up sharply at 7, by asking a blessing on the food. Right on target, Terry took her cue and slid the doors open, revealing the dining room table set and ready for us. Hungrily merging into the adjoining room, we sat down at the big table and began digging into our hot oatmeal. A large tea kettle was passed around the table, with two teabag strings hanging out under the lid. This provided a weak but warming brew for the 12 of us. Everyone seemed in good spirits at breakfast.

"We eat like kings around here!" Ted quipped, heartily washing down his oatmeal with tea. Several brothers raised their cups in agreement.

After breakfast, everyone drifted away from the table and into their rooms to get ready for work. Jon, Ted and Jay staffed the Noah's Ark Leatherworks and always walked the seven blocks to the shop, leaving by 8 a.m. They often took unemployed brothers with them to Noah's Ark, ensuring that no one would hang around the house when they should be working. In fact, house rule stated that *all* men had to be out of the house by 8, either to work, or to look for work if they didn't have a job yet. That way the sisters, who were "keepers at home," could function throughout the day without any men under foot.

That morning I needed to take Don to work so I could use our car for my first kitchen steward, grocery-shopping trip. Don changed into his work uniform and I quickly pulled on jeans and a sweatshirt, then I rapped gently on Ann and Terry's door.

"Allo, what's this?" Terry sang out in her exaggerated British accent, while opening the door. Her father was Canadian and her mother English, thus she delighted us with her provincial colloquialisms.

"Terry, I'm taking Don to work. Would you keep an eye on the kids in case they wake up before I get back?" I asked. "I don't hear a peep out of them yet."

"Not a problem," she chirped. Her brown hair, worn in a dated neck-length flip, bounced as she swung her head.

I dropped Don off at Reed Electric, on 26th and Vaughn, just about as far north as one could go before meeting the railroad yards and then the river. The streets running east and west in our northwest enclave were named in alphabetical order—from Burnside, the city's north/south division, northward to Wilson. Included were the names of Portland's founders—Lovejoy and Pettigrove—who allegedly flipped a coin to determine the city's name. It was a toss-up between Portland and Boston, their respective Maine and Massachusetts hometowns. Portland won. It was easy to find our way around just by knowing our ABCs. Our Hoyt Street house was six blocks north of Burnside and 14 blocks south of Vaughn.

I arrived back a few minutes later, just as Ted and Jay were leaving the house. "Have a good day!" they chimed in unison. "God bless you!"

Once in the house, I zipped up the stairs, meeting Ann on her way down. "The kids are awake," she informed me, smiling, then as she passed me she paused and turned, adding, "Have a good day! Goodbye!"

Terry came out of her room just as I opened my kids' door. "They're awake but they didn't get up," she assured me.

"Thanks," I smiled, as we said our goodbyes. She headed down-stairs to the kitchen to load the dishwasher before catching the 8:21 bus, a block and a half away. She had to start work at Meier and Frank by 9. I was impressed by everyone's cheerful disposition this morning. I wondered if they were always like this, or if they were just trying to make our first Monday more pleasant.

I found Bethany sitting on her bed talking with her dolls, while baby Benjie—completely soaked through his sleeper suit—lay on his back, kicking excitedly as I entered the room. After changing and dressing them both, then briefly nursing Benjie again, we went down to the kitchen. Sherry and her kids were already there, the children devouring their oatmeal at the table in the nook.

Ideally, the sister who cooked breakfast also did cleanup, if time allowed. If not, the lot fell to the kitchen steward, of whom it was assumed had all the time in the world, since she didn't go to work. Terry had loaded the bowls and cups before leaving, and now Sherry was wiping the dining table, kitchen counters and stove. A swinging door separated the nook from the dining room and could be held open by a kickstand at the bottom. It was now ajar.

I coaxed Bethany to eat her oatmeal by adding a little more brown sugar that I had brought from home. I had just recently started Benjie on fruit, adding it to his breast milk and Gerber rice cereal repertoire. I divided the last banana we'd brought, giving half to Bethany and mashing the rest into Benjie's cereal. I strapped Benjie into his infant seat and set it up on the table. He gobbled his breakfast down in a flash.

I soon noticed that both my kids were so enthralled by watching the other two children that I could get more things done. We had Benjie's swing set up in a corner of the dining room, so presently I put him in it. The older kids were playing nearby, so they continually cranked up the swing for him when it stopped.

After breakfast was cleaned up and out of the way, Sherry started doing some laundry and I wrote up a shopping list. I decided right off the bat that I was going to buy disposable diapers—out of our own money—now that we lived communally. There wasn't going to be enough time in a day for me to rinse, soak and launder cloth diapers, as I had been doing thus far with both babies. This was one luxury we *would* afford; a perk I felt I deserved for living here.

I consulted Sherry several times as I formed my shopping list, going over what we had on hand and what some of their typical menus were like. Jon had encouraged me to shop at the Food Co-Op on 23rd and Lovejoy, as the house had a "membership" there and he claimed it saved a lot of money.

I asked Sherry about it and she explained the terms to me. All the foods were organic and sold in bulk, which meant I'd have to bring my own jars, Tupperware and bags. Everything was sold by weight and was self-serve. I had never shopped like this before, and wasn't sure I was up to the challenge. Being a member meant you had to work at the store one eight-hour day per month in exchange for the privilege of shopping there. Also, there was a nominal $5 per month fee for membership in the co-op.

This is all very interesting, I remember thinking, but on that frigid winter morning, I was loath to go there. I was already up to my eyeballs in responsibility and didn't relish the thought of further complicating my grocery shopping.

Consequently, after putting the baby down for his morning nap and taking Sherry up on her offer to watch Bethany, as well, I made my first authoritative decision and drove off instead to the Fred Meyer's on Burnside.

Fred Meyer was the largest and most comprehensive grocery/department store chain in Oregon, with stores all over our city. I was familiar with "Freddie's" and, fortunately, there was one right in our neighborhood. I stuck to my list, buying the cheapest brand and the most economic size of every item. The initial meals I planned were the likes of macaroni and cheese, hamburger stroganoff, tuna casserole and meatloaf. I bought generic cornflakes to alternate with our hot grains.

Using our own money, I secured the disposable diapers and even splurged on a private stash of Cheetos for Don. Lickety-split, I arrived home before noon. Satisfied with my accomplishments, I had even managed to retain $6 for additional items that we might need later in the week. "Phew, I did it!" I exhaled.

As the days passed, we became comfortable with the routine of the house and found living with the other people to be enjoyable and stimulating. Occasionally there were miscommunications or minor tiffs involving someone shirking their responsibilities, but for the most part, we were a harmonious group.

Every morning at 6:30, I donned my full-length, sea-green, quilted-satin robe with the pearlized buttons (a wedding gift that seemed a bit too dressy for this informal group), brushed my thick, long hair back into a low ponytail and went downstairs for prayer or fixing breakfast.

Sometimes the baby was up and hungry right at that time, so I'd discreetly nurse him with a blanket over my shoulder during the meeting. He would accompany me to the kitchen and watch from his infant seat as I made breakfast. Bethany always stayed in bed, even if awake, playing with her dolls and patiently waiting until I came upstairs to tend her.

Although Benjie was only five months old, he usually slept through the night. I kept an ear open for his crying so I could get to him before anyone else awakened. On rare occasions Ann or

Terry, who said they enjoyed having a baby in the house, would beat me to him, change him and bring him to our door. I slept on the outside of the bed and Don on the inside, against the wall. That way I could hop out of bed and tend to the baby without disturbing him. I would either nurse Benjie in the big, red chair or bring him back to bed with me.

Our bedroom door had no lock on it—a fact that made me very uncomfortable, especially when we were having sex. Though it didn't seem to distract Don, I kept an eye keenly trained on that door, fearing that at any moment it would open to reveal household members congregated in the doorway, gawking at us.

I arranged our room so that our desk was at the foot of the bed, our sewing machine cabinet against the wall directly opposite it—so they could share a chair—and our dresser against the wall between the sewing machine and the door.

Bethany found out the hard way, by stepping on some, that there were straight pins imbedded in our bedroom's green carpet. They were all over the floor, as if someone had spilled a box of them, then decided to live with it rather than clean them up. Even my continual vacuuming and picking them out of the pile didn't rid the floor completely.

Sewing was my favorite hobby, as well as an affordable way to clothe myself and my family. A few months earlier, I had made Don a shirt out of unbleached muslin, trimmed with embroidery around its wide collar and cuffs. He had worn that shirt with pride on our trip to California over Thanksgiving.

We had just flown to Los Angeles in November to visit my family, celebrating the holiday as well as my sister's and my dad's birthdays. Now my brother, Dale, was engaged and we planned to return to California in May for the wedding.

My next project would be making light green matching jumpers for myself and Bethany to wear to the wedding. I also planned to fashion simple unbleached gauze curtains to hang on the lower halves of our bare bedroom windows. I happily anticipated my sewing time, which was usually in the afternoon while Benjie slept and Bethany played quietly on her bed.

After paying our rent each week, and our personal monthly bills, we were delighted to find that we had some money left over to save. Now we could definitely go to California in May, and we decided to drive down this time. We called my folks on my sister, Jane's, 18th birthday to discuss our plans.

Jane, who was not an Apostolic Christian Church member and thus allowed to date, excitedly told me about the roses she had received as a birthday surprise from her boyfriend. She was a cute high school senior with long, honey-blond hair, and I missesd her.

Our children were quite a hit at the house; everyone showered them with attention. Bethany got along well with Sherry's kids, even though they were older and sometimes instigated things she would not have thought of on her own. It was a fairly mild winter, with no snow, so the kids often played on the porch or on the sidewalk in front of the house. Sherry and I took turns tending them.

The house met for prayer on Saturday mornings as well, but it was a lot more relaxed. Those who worked on Saturdays started a little later, giving us time to make pancakes or eggs for breakfast. I preferred doing my grocery shopping on Saturdays, rather than Mondays as Sherry had done, and we made it a family outing.

I finally submitted to using the food co-op, so Don and I often walked there with the kids, toting our goods home in the stroller's net compartment and in Don's arms. The Noah's Ark guys nobly offered to take turns serving the required monthly work day at the co-op, for which I was grateful.

I bought the cheapest grains—oatmeal and millet at 19 cents a pound. When millet was served, the brothers would jokingly tweet like birds, for they knew its more common use was as birdseed. I took to buying powdered milk in bulk; for less than thirty cents I could make a gallon of milk. We used honey as our only sweetener for tea and coffee. The house didn't have a coffee maker, but several of the housemates kept their own private stash of instant. We used only natural, raw brown sugar for cereal and baking.

If our frugal diet lacked anything, it was mainly fresh fruits and vegetables, and when we ran short of anything, it was most often toilet paper. Oddly enough, without us ever expressing the need to anyone, these exact items would mysteriously appear on our doorstep. We often would find, upon first opening the door in the morning, a big brown grocery bag filled with items like celery, oranges, a head of lettuce and a bag of potatoes. And always there was a package of toilet paper on top.

These gifts were anonymous—and we deemed them miraculous—but one time a brother thought he caught a glimpse of an older female resident of the neighboring "halfway-house" fleeing our porch.

Two doors down from us was the rehabilitation house for the Damasch State Mental Hospital. It was a huge, attached-row frame structure, painted the darkest possible shade of gray before you'd have to call it black. Dozens of patients lived together there, adjusting to the outside world as they gradually prepared to re-enter it. Often some were seated on the expansive porch, staring, jerking, nodding or calling out to us as we passed by.

It was a bit disconcerting at first, as I didn't know how to respond to them. I wanted to be friendly, yet they scared me. If the Damasch people were our ministering angels, then it was certainly ironic, for we were supposed to be ministering to them. I began to learn to never second-guess God as I witnessed His unexpected workings within our community.

Sherry and I peacefully co-existed in the house, together with our kids, each day. We kept up on all the vacuuming, dusting and mopping of floors. Brothers were assigned their turns at cleaning bathrooms, but that rarely happened, so Sherry and I picked up the slack on the overlooked chores.

Before going to bed each night, we sisters took turns packing a sack lunch for every person who worked. Each person was allotted one sandwich—usually bologna or PBJ—and one side item of a cookie or carrot and celery sticks. Lining up twenty slices of bread on the counter and making sandwiches assembly-line-style was quite a feat.

Toward the end of January, a new sister and her young son moved in. Monica had recently become a Christian though her husband was not. She told us he made life so miserable for her that she had to leave him. She had heard of us through the Food Co-Op, of all things. Our neighborhood hosted a veritable smorgasbord of communes — ranging from Catholic to Buddhist, Holy Order of MANS to Hare Krishna. There was something for the most discriminating of religious tastes. We praised God for choosing to send her to us.

She gradually warmed up to us and became a boon to our kitchen and the housework load. With the addition of her son, Jeremiah, age 5, there were now five children in the house. We put her and her son in the tiny bedroom off the dining room, thus moving Jon down to the basement. She wore her long, wavy, black hair flowing down her back and always dressed in ankle-length skirts, never pants.

It didn't take long before Monica's husband, Jake, found out where she was "hiding," and he came to our door accusing us of harboring her. Don and some of the brothers talked with him at length that evening, and he eventually accepted the gospel of Christ into his life. I was a bit skeptical though, thinking perhaps he only did so to get in our good graces and to get his family back.

House policy allowed someone two weeks to stay before they got a job and contributed financially, and a one week grace period until they became a Christian. Jake moved in that night.

The longevity of Jake and Monica's marriage seemed dubious, and we all puzzled over what they ever could've had in common. She was gentle and soft-spoken, with a lilting, Katherine Hepburn-esque, eastern accent she had picked up from years of private boarding school. She was an avowed vegetarian and an advocate of only organic and whole grain foods.

Monica, of course, was a pacifist. Jake, on the other hand, was a tall, robust man who had recently returned from serving in Vietnam as an Army medic on the front lines. He had shaggy, sandy-blond hair, a full beard and a forthright manner. In his booming voice, he informed us that he had a staph infection he'd acquired in Vietnam, and he warned us we had better not touch him.

Jake initially didn't have a job, but within days of his arrival, he secured a position at a cardboard box factory. Naturally we were impressed by his military service and experience, as the lengthy and devastating Vietnam War had finally ended, thank God, just months earlier, with the fall of Saigon.

Gerald Ford was president now, having come into office upon Nixon's resignation following the Watergate scandal. National patriotism had turned to cynicism after enduring more than a decade of the belabored Vietnam War. But this was now America's Bicentennial year, 1976, and hope was that this celebration would bolster a surge of fresh patriotism and help our nation emerge from its "national nightmare," as Ford put it when pardoning Nixon's crimes.

Inspired by our bicentennial, the Body of Christ, nation-wide, put out a call for corporate repentance, citing our country's sin and degradation, and likening it to the downward spiral that led to the fall of the Roman Empire. Everyone believed doom was likewise looming for our nation if we did not heed the cry found in II Chronicles 7:14. It read, in part, "If my people, which are called by my name, shall humble themselves and pray... then will I hear from heaven... and will heal their land."

Late one afternoon as I was starting dinner, I heard Benjie crying in his room overhead. I asked Monica to cover for me in the kitchen while I ran upstairs to take care of him.

When I reached the landing, all four children scattered and I sensed they had been up to something. The baby was in his crib, but the slatted, front gate was down. I questioned Bethany, "Were you playing with Baby Benny?"

"No," was her meek reply.

"Were the kids playing with him?" I prodded.

"I don't know," she whimpered. As I lifted him from the bed, he howled even louder, as though in great pain. I laid him on the changing table and noticed that his right arm hung immobile at his side, while his left arm propelled normally. I carefully changed his diaper and outfit, but even the slightest touching of his right arm made him wail. I wrapped him in a blanket, securing the arm closer to his body and sat down to nurse him in the big red chair.

When Don arrived home from work, he came bounding up the stairs to our room. "There's something wrong with Benjie's right arm," I told him immediately. "He's crying differently and his arm is limp. I think maybe the kids did something to him."

"Let me see." Don touched the blanketed arm and Benjie winced. As he uncovered the arm to look at it, the baby broke from nursing at my breast and howled. "Do you think they picked him up by his arm, or maybe dropped him on it?" Don pondered, reading my mind.

I finished nursing him and laid him back in his crib, when presently we were called for dinner. Leaving the baby in bed, we came downstairs to find everyone gathered at the table.

"I hate to interrupt dinner, but there's something wrong with Benjie's arm, and we really need you guys to pray for him," I pleaded, my voice catching.

"Let me look at him," offered Jake, so I ran upstairs to get him. I carried Benjie downstairs and gingerly handed him to Don. The baby wailed; his little right arm hung limply at his side, while his left arm clung to his daddy.

Jake examined the arm, which we now noticed jutted out in an awkward twist at the elbow. "Poor baby," Jake crooned. "Let me see your little arm." He spoke soothingly as he felt around the now-swelling elbow. "Yeah," he confirmed, "He's got a broken arm. I've seen lots of broken bones in Vietnam, and he's definitely got a broken arm."

"We need you guys to pray for him," Don repeated. Everyone got up from the table and encircled us—laying hands on Don, me and the baby—and asked God for His healing touch.

Presently, I took the baby back upstairs and everyone began eating. Don followed me up. "Do you think we should go to the hospital?" he asked me, once we were in the privacy of our room.

"I don't know," I said, "but if we do, I want to go to Portland Adventist and have Dr. Miracle see him." Dr. Miracle was the kindly, Seventh-Day Adventist practitioner who had been my doctor during my pregnancy, delivery and follow-up. Since he had delivered Benjie, I trusted him. Don agreed and called Dr. Miracle's office exchange, leaving our message. We stayed upstairs, skipping dinner, while the housemates fed and tended Bethany.

When Dr. Miracle returned our call, Don explained the situation and our suspicions. Dr. Miracle advised us to bring Benjie in, saying he'd meet us at the hospital. After cautiously bundling the baby and leaving Monica with instructions for Bethany, we set off across town to Portland Adventist Hospital at 60th and Glisan.

The doctor was already waiting for us when we arrived. He briefly examined Benjie, confirming the fracture, and sent us up to another floor to get an x-ray while he prepared the plaster cast material.

Just as the elevator stopped and the door began opening, Benjie moved his immobile right arm, stopped crying, then raised the arm and clung to Don's shoulder. We both noticed this happening and looked at each other with a wide-eyed expression.

When the x-rays were done, we carried the file back down to Dr. Miracle, who then hung the pictures on the lighted display.

"Wha...?" he gasped, lifting his eyebrows as he stared at the transparencies. Squinting his eyes, he leaned in for a closer look. "There's no break now," he professed, still wearing a puzzled expression. He phoned up to x-ray, reiterating his findings, then turned to us. "I think we've just witnessed a healing. We have here a perfectly healthy right arm."

We thanked him, bundled up our happily cooing baby, and walked out into the dark, drizzly, Portland night, rejoicing.

On the drive home, I nursed the now quieted, contented Benjie, who was worn out from the ordeal and soon fell fast asleep in my arms. Arriving home, we related our story to the housemates and they rejoiced with us at God's miraculous intervention. It made quite an impression on all of us who were involved in the experience. We never did find out what had happened to Benjie, as none of the kids would fess up.

Shortly after this incident, Sherry and her children moved out, into another of the church houses. Jake, Monica and Jeremiah moved into Sherry's former room, across the landing from ours. Things calmed down a bit in the house, as Jeremiah was well behaved.

The following Sunday morning, as I was ironing Don's shirt, the iron toppled over sideways onto my left forearm. I ran downstairs to the kitchen to put ice on it. Several of the housemates gathered around and prayed over me.

In the days to come, the burn blistered, scabbed and eventually healed, leaving a three-inch scar that I have to this day. But I never had any pain from this burn. It never hurt me.

CHAPTER FOUR

ALTERNATIVES

"Hast thou found honey?" inquired the Bible verse I discovered taped to the kitchen cupboard door that bleak February morning. I strained to read the reference and then, realizing it was too dark, I set the baby carrier down and padded back to the light switch.

I had been feeding Benjie upstairs for the last half hour, when I suddenly remembered that breakfast would not make itself. I shuffled downstairs, in robe and slippers, bringing the baby with me. It was so gray outside that it looked like it was still night. It was freezing, too. The housemates were singing away behind the closed pocket doors, enjoying the warmth of the fireplace. I placed the heavy pan of water on the stove, measured out the oatmeal and waited for the water to come to a boil.

Pausing to fill the huge tea kettle at the sink, I re-read the verse, catching the remainder. "Hast thou found honey? Eat so much as is sufficient for thee, lest thou be filled therewith, and vomit it. - Proverbs 25:16." Cute, I thought. Someone's posting a scripture verse to warn us all to keep out of their private honey stash.

Opening the cupboard, I found a small jar of honey with a label on it which read "Jon." Beside it were two more jars labeled "Ted" and "Jay." Someone's gone shopping, I chuckled to myself. The guys must have invested in their own supply of honey, splitting the valuable commodity three ways.

We went through honey like crazy at the house, so apparently to ensure they would always have enough, they bought their own. Well, good, I thought. Now they'll quit bugging me about it. I bought honey for the house in a gallon bell jar that I filled at the food co-op and, at least twice daily, I transferred some into a small crock that looked like a beehive. It had a wooden dipping spoon with a spiral grooved paddle at the end, which completed the set.

As I put the bowls out on the dining room table, I pondered how ironic it was that even when one is pared down to a minimalist life-style—such as the one we led—one still found petty things to horde.

Well, we were rich in honey this morning but we were poor in tea, for looking in the tea canister, I found we had only four teabags remaining. Now they'd have their honey, but no tea to drink it in. If this was going to last us the rest of the week, I could only use one teabag this morning.

I dipped Benjie's pacifier in the honey crock and popped it back into his mouth when he started fidgeting. Honey was all the rage lately, as though our generation of honey freaks had just invented it. There was even a popular song by Judy Collins called *Cook with Honey*. I hardly even knew what honey was before moving back to Portland; now I was immersed in its many and varied uses. (People always think that California is the "cutting-edge" for trends, but I am convinced that Portland and Seattle lead the way in determining what's cool on the west coast.)

While stirring the oatmeal, I admired the progress of my herbs—parsley, basil, oregano and the likes—that were growing in assorted jam, baby food and mayonnaise jars on the window sill. A domed terrarium Monica had added to our "garden" was producing curly, green bean sprouts. Though I had heard you put them in salads, I wasn't quite convinced of their purpose. But hey, I could be as "hippie" as the next person.

While cleaning up the kitchen after breakfast, I passed out sack lunches to everyone as they headed off to work. I had been blessed this week to find day-old bread at five loaves for a dollar, so today everyone enjoyed the surprise of finding *two* sandwiches in their name-labeled brown bags. Usually they got either a bologna or

PB&J sandwich, but today they got both! (Monica objected to the white bread, of course, so she baked soy bread—buying the ingredients with their own money—for Jake's sandwiches.) My grocery budget was working out satisfactorily so far.

With the kitchen duties done for the moment, I took the baby, in his infant seat, out to the parlor and stood in front of the fire. It had died down to embers but still felt toasty.

It was sure hard to get the chill off this morning. As everyone traipsed in and out the door, they commented on the frosty conditions outside. Each time the front door opened and shut, a blast of frigid air blew through the drafty house.

Don came down the stairs with Bethany in his arms. "Look who's up," he smiled.

"Come here, Neenee. Stand by the fireplace with me," I urged, reaching for her.

"I'm taking the car today," Don said, "so I'll go start it and give it a chance to warm up." He buttoned his pea coat and pulled his Navy "watch cap" down over his ears. When he came back into the house, he asked me quietly, "Are you going to send the car insurance payment today?"

"Yeah," I nodded, "I think we have enough to cover it." We didn't have any credit cards yet, as Visa and Master Card were relatively new innovations, but we seemed to already have too much debt. We had purchased a studio portrait plan, a vacuum cleaner, a sewing machine and a set of encyclopedias—all on the "installment plan"—and it already seemed like we had been making payments on them forever.

Don made fairly good money, probably more than anyone else in the house. His job at Reed Electric, an electric motor rewinding plant, was now paying him $3.75 an hour, so he grossed $150 a week.

Reed was a small factory in an industrial area, flanked by abandoned rail yards and decaying warehouses, and overshadowed by a lofty freeway-entrance bridge. Back in 1905, when this neighborhood was fairly new, Portland hosted the Lewis and Clark Centennial Exposition on the grounds where these factories and warehouses now stood.

At that time, our northwest community had been a fashionable residential address. Several Victorian mansions still stood throughout the district, having managed somehow to escape the wrecker's ball during three-quarters of a century of urban evolution. By now, most had been converted into apartment buildings and boarding houses, and were in various stages of disrepair.

Don had a bicycle that he usually rode to work, but not when it was as cold as today. When Don and I first met, he owned an unpredictable 1966 Buick Le Sabre that he dotingly called "Ole Blue." He lugged his brown bike around everywhere, in the trunk of his Buick, to have on hand as backup. He even coined an affectionate little ditty, "Ole Blue, she break down. Ole Brown, she come 'round."

This same "Ole Brown" bicycle was now faithfully chained to the porch railings of Beth Israel. Ole Brown was a valuable asset these days. Gas prices had doubled in less than two years, due to the OPEC oil embargo, and now were averaging 56 cents a gallon!

Two years earlier, when Bethany was an infant, the political situation in the Middle East forced the American government to resort to the drastic measure of gas rationing. Gas was only available for sale to the public every other day, based on the final numeral of one's car license plate, be it odd or even. When rationing began, gas was priced around 28 cents a gallon, then it rose steadily—cent by cent—during the embargo, leveling out now at the doubled price.

We, and most of our Christian peers, had little interest or involvement in our world's current affairs. Our concern was being "filled with the Holy Spirit" and advancing the "Kingdom of God," and nothing else seemed to matter.

We had no television in the house and rarely bought a newspaper, so we had a very limited knowledge of what was going on in the world. A few housemates were in-tune with current events by listening to the radio, and some kept abreast of popular culture by infrequently going to a movie. We listened only to popular Christian music, so the emerging disco era went by basically unnoticed. Books emphasizing Holy Spirit renewal were in vogue; we were reading the likes of *Power in Praise*, Catherine Marshall's *The Helper*, and *Nine O'clock in the Morning* by John and Elizabeth Sherrill.

I always gave Don his haircuts; he hadn't been to a barber since his stint in the Navy. I bought strictly generic brands at the supermarket. All our food staples, and even bio-degradable laundry soap, were purchased in bulk at the co-op.

I honestly didn't know how we could be any more economically, environmentally and spiritually conscientious than we were currently being. But the day would soon come when it would be required of me to find out.

One Wednesday morning, at the POP Women's Bible Study, one of our elders' wives announced that we were forming a "food club" at church, to help us all with our grocery expenses—whether in communal houses or private. Foods would be purchased in bulk and stored at the church so we sisters could "shop" there on Wednesdays, when we came for Bible study. Commodities were a couple cents a pound cheaper than at our neighborhood co-op, so when Jon got wind of this, he *suggested* I shop there, hinting that money was really tight.

I figured what he really meant was that some people weren't paying their $40-a- week rent, and now it had to become my problem. I went along with the food club idea, though it was mostly grains and beans; not nearly all of my shopping could be accomplished there.

The concern was that many of the sisters were lacking in homemaking skills, and knew very little about how to shop, plan meals and cook. They had been raised by moms who indulged in the modern ways to feed their families, such as TV dinners and "pre-fab" packaged meals. The food-club gave us the opportunity to share recipes and ideas that encouraged a healthier lifestyle.

In the kitchen I now shared with Monica, new issues arose. Next to the Bible, she always had her nose in *Diet for a Small Planet*, a popular new book touting the many creative and varied uses for grains and legumes. Eating meat was frowned upon, both by the vegetarians as inhumane, and by the book's other fans as an unsustainable resource.

Monica refused to cook with meat when it was her turn to make dinner, and she urged me to do the same. She insisted I buy texturized vegetable protein, or "TVP," in lieu of hamburger for the meatloaves, soups and casseroles she would prepare when it was her turn to cook.

"Do you have to use so much onion?" I asked her one day. "Bethany will pick at it, and it doesn't do my breast milk any favors either." She had already chopped a large onion into the mix and was reaching for a second one.

"Oh, onions are good for children, and I nursed Jeremiah successfully while eating onions the whole time," she proclaimed. I was tempted to blurt out, "You also chew raw garlic and you reek of it," but I held my tongue.

"Then please, since you're making two TVP loaves, don't put any more onion in one of them," I begged. She rolled her eyes at me as if I were hopeless.

Sometimes industrial-size blocks of cheese were available to buy through the food club. We tested many dishes using cheese and bean combinations—striving to achieve what the book called "complete proteins"—on our "guinea pig" housemates. *Diet for a Small Planet* encouraged that "Beany Cheesy Chard" would be a crowd-pleaser, so I tried it out on the house one night. Everyone got such a kick out of the name that they actually requested I fix it again. Learning to live with the permeating odor of excessive flatulence, as a result of our beany diet, was just part of the deal.

On Sunday morning, Monica shyly told me it was her birthday. "Oh, good! I'll bake you a cake," I offered. "What kind do you like?"

Ever faithful to her convictions, she advised me to make it out of soy flour, and then she produced a recipe for me to use entitled "Soya Cake." Pulling her hidden tin of private-stash soy flour from the recesses of the cupboard, she trustingly handed it over to me.

"Here. You can use this for my cake. That would be a blessing," she cooed, in her dainty lilt. "After church, we'll be going out for the day."

"Well, I'll have it ready for tonight," I promised.

As she left the kitchen, I removed the lid from the tin and sniffed it. It didn't really look or smell much different from regular flour.

I made the cake in two layer pans and it turned out okay, but didn't rise as well as I had hoped. As it cooled, I set about making a frosting. Hmmm, now what would she like, I wondered. Oh, pink of course, since she's so feminine. I whipped up a lovely pink butter cream frosting, decorated the layers and placed twenty-six candles around the perimeter.

All afternoon as I worked on the cake, I was quite a hit with the housemates. They paraded in and out of the kitchen admiring the cake and, with mouths watering, begged for a taste of the frosting. Since it was Sunday and the house would not be eating dinner together, I waited until after 7, when most of the housemates would be home again, then placed the cake out on the center of the dining room table.

When Monica's little family arrived, I went through the house, calling all who were there to come into the dining room for a surprise. Gathered around the table, we all began to sing *Happy Birthday* as Jake led a smiling Monica into the room.

But as Monica's eyes lit on the pink-frosted cake with candles all a-blaze, her face suddenly contorted, and she interrupted us mid-song, shrieking at the top of her lungs, "What have you done? You've ruined it!!" She turned and fled the room, ran up the stairs and slammed her door.

I was stunned. Tears stung my eyes as I looked to Jake for an explanation. "You used red food dye," he patronized. "We can't eat red food dye. It's harmful to the human body. Don't you know that?"

Now *I* couldn't stand there any longer. I burst into tears, ran from the room and up the stairs, and slammed *my* door good and loud. I sat on our bed, sobbing my heart out. I had spent four hours working on that cake, and this was the thanks I got!

Presently Don opened the door. "Are you coming down?" he ventured.

"No," I sniffed.

"Well, do you mind if I eat some cake? Everyone else wants some, too."

"Go ahead. I *want* you all to eat it, but I'm not coming down," I choked back my tears. How could I live in this house? How could I live with these people?

I already knew the answer. Every teaching at church emphasized that living in community was vital to our becoming more like Christ. These irritating, abrasive encounters we had with others were to be viewed as the "sandpaper" which would rub off our rough edges and polish us into something beautiful and useful for the Lord's service.

The next morning, knowing there was no way I could avoid Monica, I plunged right in and apologized profusely, giving her a hug. She, too, apologized and we made a pact to be more sensitive to each others' needs and feelings.

As I cleaned the stovetop, I paused to consider the scripture verse hanging on the wall above it. I had read it before, but today it took on a more personal meaning. The rugged piece of wood bore a lovely hand-painted calligraphy restating John 12:24. It read, "Unless a kernel of wheat falls into the ground and dies, it produces no fruit."

Living in community was a sure-fire way to speed up this process of "dying to self," and thereby bringing forth fruit for His service. One was *forced* to become more selfless, flexible and tolerant. Our only intention in life was to become changed into the likeness of Christ; nothing else mattered, or at least nothing else was supposed to.

The emphasis of life in the house could be summed up in two simple—but certainly not easy—objectives: bringing the lost to Christ, and discipling the "newborn babes in Christ" to help them mature. Our house was like a spiritual delivery room and nursery as we aided in the birthing and raising of new Christians.

Don and I were totally committed to this concept and figured everyone else in the house was, too. Otherwise, why would they be here? The winds of doctrine were blowing in that direction. There was an urgency to the times and imminence in the current events. It was predicted that in 1987 the planets would align causing cataclysmic changes on the earth, which we believed would usher in the return of Christ and the end of the world. There was no time to waste, and certainly no time to indulge the "flesh" in its petty, materialistic desires. We must die to our flesh, and soon. Living at Beth Israel would certainly help.

Our simplistic and anti-worldly mindset was formed, not so much from being hippies or counter-culturalists, which Don and I weren't. Instead, it was born of our Apostolic Christian Church history, bred in its Anabaptist heritage of revolutionary non-conformism, which our predecessors had taken to the extreme of martyrdom. This sect taught that Christians should "not be conformed to this world," but instead be a "peculiar" and "separate" people. We hadn't had the time to be weaned gradually from our ACC ways, so we carried many of our familiar and favorite doctrines with us. The Prince of Peace merely contributed its bent.

We still didn't "believe in" owning a television which, thankfully, was a non-issue since no one else at Beth Israel had one either. I wore no makeup or jewelry—not even a wedding ring—as these were not allowed in the Apostolic Christian Church. In our desire to be faithful members, we had obeyed all their mandates and embraced their main objective, which was to be the opposite of the "world."

Weddings are just one instance where their contrasting views become sharply evident. In the "world," a bride wears a white, floor-length gown and a bridal veil, carries a bouquet of flowers, and walks in on her father's arm to the strains of an instrumental wedding march. In our wedding, I wore a knee-length dress, the customary ACC black "veil" (a six-inch wide, shoulder-length, lace strip which is worn by every female member during church services), carried a small Bible and walked in alone to the congregation's a cappella singing from their hymnals. To further ensure their understatedness, weddings are held inconspicuously during the Sunday afternoon church service, so as not to draw attention to one's self.

Female members' hair was to be long—but not worn loose and flowing—as, again, that would signify pride and the drawing of attention. I wore my long, brown hair up in a tidy bun, off my neck and face. We were further required to wear a "head covering" when we prayed. My mother set the example for me, in that, if in the course of the day she happened to not be wearing anything on her head, she would place her hands—with fingers interlocked—as a substitute, atop her bowed head when praying before a meal. I did the same.

This doctrine's viability seemed a bit vague, having to do with a verse in I Corinthians 11 about a woman needing "power on her head because of the angels," but I submitted to it and its subjugated implications. Luckily, a bandana tied behind the hair was a fashion trend now, so I easily transitioned to wearing that as my head covering.

Ours was a very sexist world, as we believed—both in the ACC and at the POP—that women were to have absolutely no authority over men. On the cusp of the feminist movement, as it was only beginning to infiltrate our world, naturally, we were against it.

As with the bandanas, once again the styles of the day were in my favor, for dress hemlines had recently lengthened, relieving us from the problematic mini-skirt.

My current wardrobe consisted of ankle-length, a-line or gathered skirts, smocked tunics and "peasant" blouses (with turtlenecks worn under them in chilly Portland), flare-leg pants, jeans and Earth shoes. Earth brand was a trendy, ergonomically-correct style of shoe where the heel was lower than the sole for the sake of achieving better posture. I owned only one pair of shoes—navy-blue suede, t-strap Earth shoes. They cost three times as much as mediocre shoes, but were well worth it for the statement they made. Besides, they were utilitarian; I wore them every day.

The house was growing. We often came downstairs to find new people in the parlor at our morning prayer meetings. On Sunday mornings we were consistently surprised by new faces at the breakfast table, most of whom had been brought home from Noah's Ark Coffeehouse the night before.

Although transients and short-term visitors made up the majority of our guests, we did add a permanent new brother named Jerry who was given a job at the leather shop. Shortly after that, a sister named Kathy arrived, moving into Terry and Ann's room. Kathy was a beautician so, as a benefit to the house, she offered to cut all the brothers' hair.

Everyone was supposed to be responsible for doing their own laundry, but one day I noticed the laundry area in the basement was becoming a vast sea of dirty, stinky clothing and bedding. Rather than resort to wearing hip boots to wade through the disgusting mess, I decided to tackle the job of catching up on all this laundry before it got completely out of hand.

It took me several days to complete the project: washing, drying and folding all these items, then stacking them neatly in boxes that I lined up along the wall at the bottom of the stairs. I informed all the housemates of my services and gave them one week to look through the boxes and claim their items.

The following Saturday, just as I had warned, Don and I carted the remaining boxes of clothes to the thrift store on 23rd. It was my equivalent of "spring cleaning." Once the basement floor was visible again, I plied the broom around the perimeter, satisfied that I'd gotten everyone off to a clean start with their clothing and bedding.

When Don's birthday rolled around, I knew I dare not make a cake with colored frosting. Instead, I fashioned a carrot-raisin cake—using both soy and whole wheat flours—baked it in a 13x9 pan and slathered it with rich, cream cheese icing. It was quite the hit, crossing all partisan lines. I divided it sixteen ways, giving everyone a good-sized serving.

Everything I made was for the entire house; I never privately cooked or baked for just our family. I delightedly discovered that a half gallon of ice cream, if rationed out carefully, could serve sixteen people one modest scoop each. Most of the guys, so accustomed to scant rations, were thrilled when I would answer yes to their question, "Should we save our spoons?" That meant we were having dessert! A scoop of ice cream went a long way in pleasing them so, when Freddie's had their store-brand half gallons on sale for 49 cents, I stocked up.

I got Don a store-bought shirt from Fred Meyer's for his birthday. It was unbleached muslin with a pale green-sprigged print, and it fastened with white pearlized snaps instead of buttons. He looked really cool in it. But unfortunately for Don, turning 24 also required a trip to the dentist.

For several weeks Don had been complaining of toothaches on both sides of his jaw. We decided he had to find out what was wrong, whether we could afford it or not. His diagnosis was that his two lower wisdom teeth were impacted, and the two upper ones would become so, also, if they weren't removed soon. He opted for the surgery.

At one appointment he had the two on the left side removed and then, two weeks later, the two on the right. He was in a great deal of pain, with each cheek swollen for a long time. He stuffed his cheeks with cotton pads to soak up the blood and drool. Everyone called him "chipmunk cheeks" and, when forced to laugh, he cradled his distorted face in his hands. Day and night he moaned while sopping up the drainage that seeped from the corners of his mouth. Poor Don.

The house prayed over him for a healing several times, considerably more than they had for Benjie, but this time we didn't witness God's intervention. Don struggled through the month of March with intense pain and discomfort.

On the other hand, there almost seemed to be an aura around our son. During my pregnancy, many people had offered to pray for the baby in my womb. Several prophesied over him that he would become a "mighty man of God." Even complete strangers had approached me and offered a blessing on my unborn child. We now viewed the miraculous way God had healed his broken arm to be a reinforcement of this.

Both our children were favored by the housemates. Bethany was plump and adorable with her wide, blue eyes and silky, brown hair with bangs. She was smart as a whip at two—able to sing songs and "read" her favorite story books by memory—to the amazement of the adults. Benjie had flirtatious, brown eyes and his hair was coming in thick and blond. Their individual appeal endeared them to the members of the house.

With Easter approaching, I wanted to somehow make the holiday festive for all the housemates. Our little family was going to be at my aunt and uncle's for Easter dinner, and most of the others were invited somewhere else, too. Since Easter Sunday was a free day for dinner, I decided instead to plan a special Sunday morning breakfast for the house.

On Saturday evening, I boiled, colored and decorated Easter eggs just as if we were in our own home. Bethany had such fun coloring the eggs with me. At two years old, she could participate much more than she had the previous year. I prepared three dozen eggs to ensure each person would get two, as now there were 18 people living in the house. Most of the housemates, including Don, were out that evening, or at the coffeehouse, so few knew what I was up to. I was glad because I wanted it to be a special surprise in order to bless them and make Beth Israel feel homier.

I emptied the magazines from a basket in our room, placed a piece of floral, pastel fabric in it and brought it down to the kitchen. After they dried, Bethany helped me carefully place all thirty-six eggs into the basket. We set the basket up on the top shelf in the refrigerator, with a sign taped to it saying "Keep Out 'Til Breakfast!"

Terry was scheduled to make breakfast Sunday, but was spending the night with her parents. I trusted she would be home early in the morning to fulfill her duty, so I wrote her a note telling about the Easter eggs I had made. Now all she would have to do that hectic Sunday morning was make juice and toast to go with them.

The next morning, after dressing up in our Easter best, Don and I ambled cheerfully downstairs and into the kitchen, our children in tow. We were totally unprepared for what would ensue.

Terry stood at the sink, her back to us, as we came into the room. We sang out a friendly greeting, "Good morning! Happy Easter!" as we set the infant seat on the nook table and situated Bethany in her booster chair.

Terry twirled around to face us. "How could you do this??" she shouted. "You've insulted my convictions!" Her face was red from crying, swollen with tears. "I can't serve these eggs to a Christian house! Easter eggs are a *pagan* practice!" She wheeled back around, pretending to busy herself at the sink. Her words seemed to echo off the walls, the tension reverberating throughout the room.

I couldn't believe my ears. I had done it again. But this time it was ridiculous. "I've, I've always done Easter eggs," I stammered, tears forming in my eyes, "and I don't believe there's anything wrong with them."

"We're okay with Easter eggs," Don backed me up. "Judy thought everyone would appreciate it."

Terry turned her head slightly toward us, mercilessly wringing a dish towel as she seethed, "Well whether they eat them or not is up to each person's conscience, but I, for one, am having nothing to do with it!" She threw the twisted towel into the sink, turned with a huff and marched out of the room.

I was tempted to cut and run myself, but I was determined to maintain my composure better than I had in the Monica incident. I continued going through the motions of preparing my family's breakfast, but my hands were shaking and I couldn't speak without my voice cracking. For my family's sake, I smiled and feigned light-hearted small-talk while we ate our Easter eggs, privately, at the kitchen nook table.

There were so many things to learn here. The concrete house rules were easy to heed: no alcohol, no cigarettes, no drugs and no sex outside of marriage. It was the unknown, unexpected, gray areas that got one into trouble. The picayune legalisms of "straining at the gnat" or "tithing on herb leaves" were what Jesus warned would breed discord.

When we finished breakfast, no one was in the parlor—thank goodness—so I slipped in and sat on my rocker to nurse Benjie. Don put a *2nd Chapter of Acts* record on the stereo and we listened to the beautiful strains of their *Easter Song*, "He's risen, hallelujah...," as we recomposed ourselves for a few minutes before leaving for church.

The sun was coming out. As it filtered through the leaded glass of the parlor window, it refracted dancing, elfin rainbows on the floor, the walls, and on me and my family.

Don—in his new birthday shirt—holding Benjamin,
shortly after the healing of the baby's right arm.

CHAPTER FIVE

TESTING

The next morning, I was still a bit shell-shocked by Terry's incendiary objection to the Easter eggs. She offered no apology and acted as though nothing had happened. I figured this must be her way of dealing with it, so I decided to follow suit. I didn't believe I had to apologize this time because, honestly, I had done nothing wrong. I determined not to bring up the topic either.

Those who bore no conviction against the Easter eggs continued to eat them, discreetly, when Terry wasn't around. Several of the brothers privately asked me if they could take them in their lunch, and our family ate them, so it was only a matter of days until the house was rid of the offensive objects. I amused myself imagining what her reaction might have been had I turned the remainder into "deviled eggs."

We sisters, at Terry's suggestion, decided to start our own Bible study, one morning a week. We would meet on Friday mornings, right after breakfast was cleaned up and the brothers had all gone to work. On Fridays, Terry and Kathy didn't have to be at work until 10, so the only one unable to attend was Ann, as she left for her teaching job by 8 each morning.

Our first meeting was successful, with Monica, Kathy, Terry and I all present. We decided that our format would be to take turns bringing a devotional or a reading, and then allow time for sharing and personal prayer needs.

It was strange because Terry acted as if our altercation had never occurred and, in fact, she was more gracious toward me than ever before. As I got to know her, I was delighted to find she had a great sense of humor, and I appreciated the friendship we were developing. She loved our kids and showered them with attention.

She had several stuffed animals on her bed and allowed the children to play with them during our meetings. Bethany was especially fond of a lanky, life-size, stuffed black cat that Terry affectionately called Samuel. Samuel—named for the Old Testament prophet—was soft and flexible, about the size of a newborn infant. Terry had him dressed in a white, newborn-size "onesie" and light-blue, pinwale, corduroy overalls. Bethany never tired of dressing and undressing that cat.

To ensure that she had enough time to prepare for work, Terry suggested we hold our meetings in her room while she got dressed, if we didn't mind. It was an interesting assemblage of three women sitting on beds—one of them nursing an infant—two small children playing nonchalantly with stuffed animals on the floor, while a fourth woman went through all the stages of getting dressed. Terry wore more conservative attire than the rest of us—almost matronly—suitable for clerking at a high-end department store. This scenario wasn't too odd or embarrassing for me, though, as I had grown up sharing a bedroom with my two sisters.

The following Friday morning, shortly after Terry and Kathy left for work and Monica took her son out for a walk, a girl about my age knocked at the door. She arrived on a bicycle and had wheeled it up the stoop onto the porch. She wore a backpack over a coarsely woven poncho, flare-leg jeans with embroidered trim, and her long, brown hair was in a neat braid hanging down her back.

As she spoke, she held onto the bike's handle bars with one hand, while removing elastic bands from her ankles with the other. I assumed these were to prevent her flared pant legs from getting tangled in the bike's chain. She shook each leg, allowing the wide bells to unwrinkle and hang freely over her worn, brown, oxford Earth shoes.

Without giving her name, she introduced herself as a student at Portland State University, and then she got right to the point. "Some people on campus told me I could come here to get saved," she announced.

I was taken aback. Faltering at her directness, I asked, "Uh, you mean you want to know about God's plan of salvation through Jesus?"

"Sure, tell me about Jesus."

I stood there not knowing how to react to her matter-of-factness. I had never seen this before. Usually someone had to be cautiously introduced to the topic, convinced of its truth, and finally coached into receiving Christ.

I was uncomfortable with evangelism, personally, feeling my gifts were more along the serving and hospitality lines. Don, on the other hand, was bold and well-versed in leading someone to the Lord. I suddenly felt flooded with fear, realizing there was no one else at home right now to help me. I was alone and God had brought this seeking soul to my doorstep.

"Um, okay, come on in," I offered. She did so, and sat down cross-legged on the parlor floor. I sat down on the rocker, arranged my wrap-around floral skirt, and placed the baby in the infant seat at my feet. Bethany was playing nearby in the dining room. "Do you want some tea?" I suggested. It was the great leveler of society.

She nodded, so I went out to the kitchen, thankful to find the tea kettle still simmering from breakfast. I splurged, putting a new teabag into a cup just for her.

I carried the cup of tea and the honey back into the parlor. "Honey?" I asked, extending the hive-shaped crock. She nodded and accepted it. That was a given.

Glancing around the room, I located my Bible, which, thankfully, was still on the coffee table from our morning prayer meeting. I sat down and opened it with trembling hands. Inside, on the front blank page, I found my hand-written notes of scriptures to use when leading someone to the Lord. This would be my first occasion to use this material.

At the top of the page I had outlined the "Four Spiritual Laws" from a popular witnessing tract. Further down, I had listed the "Roman Road" references which my aunt had recently given me. Bless you, auntie, I prayed. This outline consisted of five verses— all found in the New Testament book of Romans—that if used in a progression, could adequately present the gospel and lead one to the point of accepting Christ into their life.

I nervously began. "God sent His Son, Jesus, to provide a way for our salvation." I had no idea how much time she had. I wondered if I should hurry through this because she may have a class to get to. Or should I go into more detail so she would have a better foundation? My mind pleaded, oh, where is Don when I need him?

"Um, it says here in Romans 3:23 that we are all sinners," I fumbled at the thin pages until I found the passage, and then read it to her.

"Right," was all she said.

I continued, "In Romans 6:23, it says that the wages of sin is death." Gulp. I wished my hands would stop shaking. "But here in Romans 5:8, it says that God made a way for us, because while we were yet sinners, Christ died for us." I paused, looking up from the Bible, into her face. "Do you believe this?"

"Yes," she nodded her head. This was way too easy.

"Umm, in uh, Romans 10:9 it says that if you believe this in your heart and confess it with your mouth, you'll be saved," I smiled, biddingly, feeling a bit more at ease now. "Verse 13 says that whoever calls on the name of the Lord will be saved." I looked at her for my next cue. "Would you like me to pray with you, and you can ask Jesus into your heart?"

"Yes, I would," she said softly, and I noticed that tears stood in her eyes. I got off the rocker and knelt down on the carpet in front of her. Taking her hands in mine, I reiterated the five verses in prayer to God, with her agreeing. She closed with a brief sentence, thanking God for forgiving her sins and coming into her heart.

We stood to our feet and I gave her a big hug. "You're my sister in Christ now," I smiled.

She paused at the door and turned to hug me in return, then thanked me as she leaned over to replace the elastic bands around her ankles. Climbing into her backpack, she adjusted her shoulder straps and wheeled her bike down our stairs to the sidewalk.

Oh! I had almost forgotten. "Be sure to find other Christians to hang out with," I called after her, waving. She returned the wave and then peddled off westward, up Hoyt Street.

I closed the door, came back into the parlor and sat down. I was in a daze; it all seemed so surreal. Had this actually happened? Had God brought her to me as a test or to strengthen my spiritual muscles? It seemed like bad timing that I was the only one home to talk with her. Surely someone else would've done a much better job.

God certainly knew I needed the practice and perhaps He used this incident so I could gain self-confidence. But maybe it wasn't about me at all. God knew her heart was ready, so He brought her to the closest place. My mind swam with all the possibilities.

Perhaps, I was really "entertaining an angel unaware," as the passage in Hebrews 13 suggests. I felt a little spooked by that explanation, but a warm, comforting presence of the Holy Spirit enveloped me for the remainder of the day.

On the evening of our third wedding anniversary, the housemates surprised us with a card they had all signed and two store-bought cupcakes, each with white icing and a candle in it. Terry lit them and brought them out to us as everyone finished dinner. Around the dining room table, they all joined in singing a rousing rendition of *Happy Anniversary*, then proceeded to razz us about whether we were really married or not.

"You aren't wearing wedding rings," someone pointed out, tauntingly.

"The church we got married in didn't allow wedding rings, so we've never had them," I explained, a bit defensively. Then loosening up, I quipped right back at them, "I've already gone through two pregnancies without a wedding ring. There's nothing you guys can say that's more intimidating than that!"

"You don't have to have wedding rings to be married," Don added. "We had a real wedding, so we're really married."

Another housemate joined in, "Maybe you're not *really* married, though; maybe you're just living together."

"We're thinking about getting rings soon," Don affirmed. "We *are* really married." I could tell he was getting a bit annoyed by the continuance of the topic.

"If you want proof that we're married, I'll show you our wedding pictures," I piped up, then ran upstairs to find our photo album. Opening it to our wedding pictures, I passed the book around the table. But now I was stuck with explaining why we had such a goofy-looking wedding.

"The church we were in also doesn't allow floor-length gowns, so that's why I had to wear a knee-length dress," I explained, then added, "I made it myself."

I continued relating some of the other oddities: no photography allowed inside the church building, no carrying of a bouquet and no music. "But," I added, "We attempted to personalize it as much as possible. We *did* write our own invitations and I selected the color and style of our bridesmaids' and servers' dresses."

Once my out-of-state attendants had arrived, we worked together at making their headpieces and bouquets. Unassuming floral bouquets and bridal veils were allowed only at the reception, as it was in a home and not in the church building. I had insisted on making my dress out of white satin, thus slightly bucking the Apostolic Christian Church system which favored off-white or pastel dresses, again, differing from the "world."

Finally, I guess we convinced them that we were legal, but now we had exposed our unusual background. We probably should get wedding rings soon, I thought, at least to be a better witness to everyone. The "living together" trend was gaining momentum and we certainly didn't want our relationship misrepresented. We weren't about to tell the housemates, but we were saving money for rings, as well as other personal needs that were upcoming.

A couple weeks later, after saving aside enough money, Don and I belatedly celebrated our anniversary at *der Rheinlander*. Terry and Ann babysat our kids while we enjoyed a special dinner alone at one of Portland's landmark German restaurants.

We enjoyed a delicious cheese-and-beer fondue accompanied by a variety of German breads for dipping. Eating out was such a rarity that we truly savored the sauerbraten, bratwurst, kraut and schnitzel—then splurged at the end by sharing a piece of decadent, Black Forest, cherry-chocolate cake. For a couple of hours, we almost forgot we would have to return home to a house full of half-starved, half-crazed hippies.

Don and I scarcely had any private time together. The needs of the house always came first, and they were legion. Don was called upon to counsel people, day or night, and I tired of constantly sharing my husband. It seemed we were always conversing with someone, but never with each other. We needed to check in with each other from time to time, or we could lose sight of the importance of our marriage and family in the light of the distractions of ministry.

I don't think it bothered him as much as it did me, for men seem to thrive on being busy and in demand; it boosts their egos. But tonight was our special time together. I had him all to myself. Ironically, we could hardly think of anything to discuss that didn't lead the conversation right back to the kids or the house.

"We probably should buy wedding rings soon," I broached the topic.

"Yeah, I didn't think it would be such a big deal. Maybe we can get them after we get back from California. We'll have to see how much money we have left," Don agreed.

We talked about our plans to drive down to California in May for my brother's wedding. We decided we would also go to the San Diego area to see Don's relatives this time. And we discussed going to Disneyland if my mom could baby-sit Benjie for us. He was too young to take there, but Bethany was old enough to enjoy it.

We arrived home to a quiet house and went upstairs to find Bethany sound asleep and the baby stirring, as it was time for his 10 p.m. feeding. I thanked Ann, as she peeked out her bedroom door to let us know all had gone well with the kids. After changing and nursing Benjie, I tucked them both in securely and returned to our room.

Don was almost asleep. I joined him in bed and we laid there whispering for a few minutes, reminiscing about how far we had come in just three short years of marriage. We had two children, had lived in three different homes, in two states, and now were responsible for the 16 people under this roof. We drifted off to sleep, thinking about the varied and unexpected ways God was directing our lives. We were in awe of Him.

The phone was ringing. I rolled over and sat up as it rang again. I knew no one else was going to get it; no one ever did when it rang in the middle of the night. Did everyone really sleep that soundly, I wondered, or were they just faking it because they didn't want to get up? I didn't want the phone to wake the baby, because he would cry and want to be nursed again. I would never get any sleep.

It kept on ringing as I got out of bed and slipped on my bath-robe. We occasionally got phone calls in the middle of the night at the house, but they were usually wrong numbers or prank callers. I got up anyway, thinking there was always the chance it could be an emergency call from a family member in California. That incentive—and wanting to prevent the phone from waking the baby—kept me headed toward the shrill menace on the table in the landing.

I shivered as I quietly shut the bedroom door behind me, realizing how frigid it was on the landing. I lifted the receiver, stopping the incessant din, and then balancing the phone between my jaw and shoulder, I continued buttoning up my robe to keep out the draft.

"Hullo," I murmured, praying my kids had not awakened. At first there was no sound, but as I transferred the receiver into my left hand, I heard a woman's laughter. Oh great, I thought, another prank call. "You're not funny," I told the caller. "Don't call here again."

I was about to hang up, but the female voice said, "Wait! Don't hang up." Continuing to giggle, she added, "There's something I need to tell you."

"Who is this?" I demanded.

"Oh, you don't know me, Hon, but you know a friend of mine." She laughed again.

I groggily repeated, "Don't call here anymore. It's the middle of the night. There are children sleeping." I was not amused. I glanced over at the digital clock on the table; its red numerals glowed 2:14.

"But there's something you need to know…" she started.

"What are you talking about? Who do you need?" I interrupted.

"I'm talking about my friend," she snickered. "He's right here with me, ya know. He's with me lots of nights, ya see, and we have all kinds of fun together. We play little games, ya know. Sex games. And he pays me, ya know. So now you know what that makes me, right Hon?"

All my instincts were screaming at me to hang up on her. I couldn't believe my ears! Now I had an obscene phone call to deal with, and from a woman, no less. I don't know why I stayed on the line. "You're not with any friend of *mine*," I answered, dryly, "so don't call here again."

"Oh, but I am, Hon," her laugh became husky now, as if she was ready to reveal more. She paused and then in a quieter tone confided, "I'm with your pastor."

"That's not true," I countered. "I rebuke you in the name of Jesus, and I command you, in the name of Jesus, to not spread lies and to not call here again!" I broke into praying in tongues under my breath. How dare this person call here telling these abominable lies?

I realized I was shaking all over, partly from the chilliness, mostly from the emotional stress. My hand was trembling so violently I could barely hold the telephone receiver to my left ear. With a quivering voice, I attempted to form an intelligible prayer, in spite of the duress.

I was about to remove the receiver from my ear when I heard her begin breathlessly describing the things they were doing together, where he was touching her, etc. "Don't hang up," she panted, apparently sensing I was about to. "I'll prove to you that I'm with your pastor." She paused and caught her breath. "His name is Willard, and right now he's..." Her voice trailed off into gales of giggles.

My heart leaped into my throat and I tightly gripped the phone table to keep from falling over. "That's not true!" I told the telephone, gasping for breath. I held the receiver away from my face with a trembling hand, staring at it in disbelief, as she continued describing the intimate acts she and Willard were engaged in.

"I rebuke you, in the name of Jesus," I attempted again. "Satan is the accuser of the brethren! Stop telling these lies about our brother, in the name of Jesus!"

Again I held the phone away from me, staring at it as though I couldn't think of what to do with it. Blood rushed to my head, causing my pulse to pound so loudly that I was sure the other occupants of the second floor could hear it.

Don opened our bedroom door and frowned at me, concerned and questioning. "Who is it?" he whispered. "What's going on?"

"It's some woman telling horrible lies about Willard," I breathed.

He walked over and taking the phone from my hand, he, in like manner, firmly denounced the caller. "In the name of Jesus, I rebuke you. Stop telling lies about our brother in Christ. Satan is the accuser of the brethren," he ensued. "Satan, we cast down your vain attempts to destroy our brother, in the name of Jesus!" He replaced the receiver on its cradle and escorted me back into our room.

"She might try calling again," I whispered, "or maybe she'll call other houses or people from church. I have no idea how she got this number; she might have others." Beth Israel and Noah's Ark were listed separately from the Prince of Peace in the phone book, under the heading of Northwest Fellowship.

Don returned to the landing and brought the telephone into our room. Its extension cord was long enough to allow it to reach into any of the four bedrooms on the second floor and most of the way up the attic stairs.

We shut our door to maintain privacy and sat down on the edge of our bed, with the phone on the floor at our feet, wondering what to do next. I was so stunned that I just sat there staring at a spot of light that beamed through the window onto the dark carpet.

"You're right," Don finally said. "She may try calling again or call other houses to spread these lies. I think I better call Chuck and warn him." Chuck was one of the assistant pastors, and we knew his number by heart. I felt bad having to call his house at 2:30 in the morning, perhaps waking his family, but this was serious.

After several rings, Chuck's sleepy voice answered, "Hullo."

"Chuck, this is Don Cremer," said my husband. "I'm sorry to bother you at this hour, but it's important. A woman just called here saying she's a prostitute, and that she's with Willard. I wanted to warn you in case she called you or someone else from church, to spread her lies."

There was a long, belabored silence on the other end of the line. Slowly Chuck drew in his breath and said, softly, "There are some issues of immorality regarding Willard, but it's late. We'll talk tomorrow, brother."

As if in slow motion, Don deliberately set the receiver back on its cradle and turned to face me. We sat quietly staring at each other as moonlight shone through the window, casting pallor on our already ashen faces.

So it was true.

We didn't know how to process this information. Don quietly wrestled the phone and its 25-foot cord back to the table in the landing, returned to our room and shut the door. Apparently no one else, including our children, had awakened.

We laid in bed wide awake for a long time, each consumed by our own thoughts. I wondered why Willard would have allowed her to make that phone call. Maybe it was a game they were playing, or a dare. Maybe he was drunk or high. Or perhaps he was at the point where he didn't care any more and actually wanted to be found out.

We were well-versed in loyally defending the brethren against the accusations of the evil one. But now, what we feared most had come upon us; the accusations were true.

CHAPTER SIX

CHANGES

During the remains of the night, while attempting a fitful sleep at best, the phone call kept replaying in my mind like a broken record. Shortly before dawn a wind whipped up, strong enough to rattle the window panes as it whistled around the corners of our aged edifice. This north edge of the city seemed to get pounded by the raw winds blowing in off the Columbia River. When we lived out in the southeast area, we weathered the gusts that funneled through the Columbia Gorge but, I decided, these northwest winds were even worse.

A scripture verse came to me and, though I didn't know its reference, it clung to the webby recesses of my mind as I passed in and out of sleep. It went something like "He who brings trouble upon his own house will inherit the wind." I could not even begin to imagine the far-reaching trouble Willard's actions would bring.

When the baby awoke crying at daybreak, I felt sure I had just fallen asleep. I sat in the big, red chair, woozily looking out the window as I nursed. The gradually lightening sky was a murky gray, with vertical silvery rays, indicating sheets of rain were rapidly blowing in.

Then momentarily, the storm was upon us. A flash of lightning pierced the sky, followed by an intense boom of thunder that rumbled and reverberated, shaking the house. I thought of a teaching that Chuck had recently given at church. He said that sometimes great shakings come in life, so strong that anything that can be shaken will be shaken. Only the faith that is strong enough to endure the shaking will be the faith that remains.

I wondered how anyone's faith could remain now, as we would be dealing with the fall of our beloved pastor. We were groping our way into unfamiliar territory.

We went through the motions of getting ready for church and preparing breakfast, all the while hiding our feelings of numbness inside. Apparently, no one else had heard the phone call in the night, or if they did, they mercifully didn't mention it.

Maybe it was all a terrible nightmare, I mused, but when I looked at Don's troubled face, I knew we weren't that lucky. Perhaps God had shielded all the other housemates from receiving the phone call. Oh, great, I thought, that must mean He thinks we're mature enough to handle it. Just what we *don't* need, I sighed, is more responsibility. Then I remembered the verse that says, "To whom much is given, much is required."

The storm intensified as we ate breakfast, and by the time we all fled the house, clamoring into cars to go to church, it was raining in torrents. Downtown Portland appeared to be drowning as we carefully maneuvered through the swollen streets.

Church was packed that morning, in spite of the foul weather. There seemed to be an influx of new people—hippies and unkempt for the most part—understandably looking a bit worse for wear due to the storm. We crammed together like sardines into the century-old, wooden pews, and when there was no more seating space, several walked up front and sat cross-legged on the floor. It was a motley crew, an unorthodox-looking assemblage for a church.

Thunder, lightning and the loud spattering of rain against the ancient structure all joined in accompanying the congregation in their worship. One sister suggested we sing a favorite, *Our God Reigns*, adding that we should change it to "Our God R-A-I-N-S!" Everyone laughed as we began belting out a rousing rendition. When the Prince of Peace Band started playing, Mary's lovely voice rose with clarity *a la* Joan Baez, and Chuck's trumpet blared, all voices joined in a praise that resonated from the rafters.

Not surprisingly, Willard and his wife were not there that morning and nothing was mentioned about him during the service. Briefly, after church, Chuck took Don aside and assured him that the elders would be meeting with Willard soon. He guaranteed that the situation was being handled with delicacy and in the spirit of New Testament love and discipline. Apparently mum was the word, but Don and I weren't about to mention it to anyone, regardless.

During the next few days, even though our housemates may not have known of Willard's transgression, it seemed they may have sensed it in the spirit, as a strained feeling permeated the house. Our once harmonious flow was now at ebb. For instance, when I approached Jon for a little additional money for some household supplies, I was reprimanded for not being able to make ends meet.

Out of necessity one evening, Don and I took the kids with us on a little walk to Fred Meyer's and purchased the needed items with our own money. I redeemed some coupons I had clipped from an occasional Sunday *Oregonian* we bought at the newsstand on the corner of 23rd.

Taking these walks gave us an opportunity to discuss topics together, away from the interruptions and eavesdropping of the house. Don and I, still fresh from the Apostolic Christian Church, could barely fathom the concept that Christians weren't perfect and sinless after their conversion and salvation experience. Admittedly, we were judgmental back then and had a difficult time processing Willard's fall into such blatant duplicity. He was such a gifted man and a godly example—having a wonderful wife, grown children, even young grandchildren. How could this kind of thing happen?

The next Sunday, Willard and his wife were not at church again and still nothing was mentioned to explain his absence. But during the service, announcement was made that our church leadership would now be in the guise of a "plurality of elders." These six men were asked to stand and come up front to be introduced. This news caught most of the congregation off-guard, and there was much conjecture as to what had happened to our pastor.

One evening later that week, these elders, along with the communal house heads and a few others in leadership, held a meeting. Both Don and Jon attended from Beth Israel. When Don returned, he filled me in on all the changes we were facing, starting with the good news.

Willard and his wife would no longer be attending the Prince of Peace. He had made a full confession to the leadership and was extremely repentant. He would return the following Sunday to make his public statement to the congregation. He and his wife had begun attending a thriving Charismatic church on the east side of town, where they could find healing and enough anonymity to not feel ostracized by the body of believers there.

After discussing this for awhile, it was time for Don to dump the bad news in my lap: Starting immediately, all of the communal houses were going on the "100% system." This meant that all occupants must now give over *all* their income to the house in which they lived. The "house" (meaning Jon, in our case) would then pay each individual's bills and provide for all their needs—"having all things common"—as exemplified by the early church in the book of Acts. This concept was encouraged in current books on "discipleship" and "shepherding," by Juan Carlos Ortiz and others.

Apparently, the Prince of Peace had already implemented the 100% system once before, during a period of timer prior to our move to Beth Israel. Now they had decided to reinstate the system to ensure funding for the communal house ministry, which, next to the coffeehouses, was their predominant outreach thrust.

In return for his or her courageous step of faith, each individual housemate would be given a token weekly "allowance" at the rate of $5 per adult and $2 per child.

I tried to view this imperative with the eyes of faith, but it looked to me like there must have not been enough people working and paying rent to support the houses. Now they wanted all the earnings from all the employed people, in order to support all the unemployed people. Instead of our family unit paying the understandable $90, Don would have to sign over his entire paycheck— $140 after taxes—to the house each week. This was either going to be an experiment in faith-based living at its finest or communism at its worst.

The Prince of Peace absolutely touted the communal house lifestyle as being the most Biblical and the most conducive to Christian growth. Yet for some reason, the older, more established members were not urged to turn the homes they owned into communes, or to sell them, giving their profits to the church. Maybe I was overthinking the principle—I've been told I'm a tad too analytical for my own good—but there seemed to be a double standard operating.

Willard was a homeowner—of a very nice house, in fact—and under his leadership validity to personal income and property had been upheld. Now, in the wake of this debacle, church leadership was changing from a pastorship to a plurality of elders, with two of the elders—Chuck and Ron—emerging as salaried co-pastors. The remaining elders, lay-leaders with paying occupations elsewhere, all lived communally, save one. That one home-owning elder was my uncle.

Don and I thoroughly discussed the new system in private, and decided to submit to it. We were in no position to move out already and not wanting to look like quitters, we determined to prove our commitment. And though we would never admit it, in a small way we welcomed the challenge and anticipated seeing how God would honor our new step of faith. Maybe there was joy to be found in living sacrificially so that others could benefit.

We had managed to save a little money in the few months we lived at Beth Israel, at least enough to cover our upcoming trip to California. I also had stocked up on remnant fabrics with which to make us some additional summer clothes. Hopefully we would have enough money left to buy wedding rings, too, as the days of extra money were gone.

When Don handed his paycheck over to Jon that Friday evening, it again occurred to me that he, no doubt, earned more than anyone else in the house. But we also had more bills than anyone else, and these too we submitted to Jon. I had an uneasy feeling as we relinquished our personal affairs into public domain. Now we had to trust a young, single guy we had known for less than four months, to diligently continue making payments on our doctor bills, car insurance and portrait program. We would no longer retain the oversight of our cash flow.

At least we already had a car, and thankfully, it was paid for. We owned a pale green, 1968 Chevy Biscayne, acquired last August by evenly swapping our inoperative Chevrolet Vega. Our darling, little orange Vega, "Chevy's rising star," as it was bogusly advertised, had been my first car.

I had graduated from high school, and then was baptized in the Apostolic Christian Church in June, 1972. For the next three months I traveled: first, to Portland for a cousin's wedding; second, to Alabama for several weeks, where I helped teach Vacation Bible School; and third, to Indiana, where I stayed for the remainder of the summer with my aunt, working in her bake shop and babysitting her boys.

Upon returning home in mid-September, I began looking for my first "real" job. Our family had only one car and my dad drove it to work each day. I was expected to find a job on foot, so I spent weeks walking to literally *every* place of employment within about a one-and-a-half-mile radius of our El Monte home. I put in applications at every restaurant, store and factory. After getting no offers, I begged my dad to somehow find a way to get me a car, so I could expand my job search. Then once I was hired, I could start paying him back.

My mom had recently received a nominal inheritance settlement, from her mother's passing the year before, so my dad finally relented, saying we could use some of that money to purchase a car. We found that our local Chevrolet dealer was clearing the lot to make room for the '73 models, so we were shown a 1972 "demo" with 17,000 miles on it. My dad got the dealer to part with it for only $1,750—by offering cash on the spot, "take it or leave it."

With wheels, I was able to apply for jobs in neighboring cities and, within days, I was hired full-time at a Christian bookstore. I started working there in mid-October, at the minimum wage of $1.55 an hour. This netted me $56 each week, $50 of which I agreed to pay my dad towards the car. I pinched every penny of my remaining $6 a week, dividing it between gas, car insurance and pantyhose.

I paid Dad $50 a week for several weeks, during which time Don and I became engaged. Then in December, with Christmas approaching and wedding expenses to plan for, I had to alter it to $50 a month.

After Don and I married, in the early spring of 1973, we had rent and utilities of our own—and then a baby on the way—but we managed to continue making the $50 a month car payment for awhile.

My pregnancy, Bethany's birth, and her subsequent hernia operation all caused our payments to become more strained, for I had quit working and we had absolutely no medical insurance. We were overwhelmed by how we could ever manage to pay all those doctor bills, but somehow we worked out a way of incorporating their monthly installments into our meager budget.

By naively submitting to the Apostolic Christian Church's edict forbidding the use of any type of birth control (even though it overrode our better judgment, and we later found that many ACC couples more mature than we merely viewed it as a "don't ask, don't tell" matter), we soon found ourselves unprepared, poverty-stricken young parents, desperately paddling to stay afloat. I guess the satisfaction of knowing we were obedient to their rules was supposed to be enough to see us through. (You better believe we were using birth control now, for although we wanted more children, the last thing I needed was to find myself pregnant at Beth Israel!)

Once we were settled in Portland and Don was making more money, we resumed sending my dad $50 a month. When the Vega broke down in February, 1975, Don took out a loan to pay for the repairs and then moonlighted, with an early morning *Oregonian* paper route, in order to repay it.

Six months later, right on the heels of our leaving the Apostolic Christian Church and Benjamin's birth, our Vega developed a cracked cylinder. Mechanics advised us not to invest in a new engine, as Vegas were built to be "disposable."

Somehow we managed to coax the little car onto a Chevrolet lot. We made it clear that we had absolutely no money to buy or trade up, but when we noticed a Biscayne sedan with a window-sticker price of $600, we instigated a trade. Apparently our Vega, even in its broken-down state, was more beneficial to the lot in resale value than this Biscayne. Small cars were all the rage, due to gas prices and shortages. I'll never know how, but we miraculously finagled an even trade. The orange Vega stayed on the lot, and we drove away in the green '68 Biscayne. However, one glitch remained: the dealership needed the title to the Vega and my dad had it, because we still owed him $180.

My dad dealt the final control card in his hand and refused to sign the title over to us until we paid him off in full. We had to have the title and certainly didn't have a spare $180, so we explained the situation to my uncle, the Prince of Peace elder. We asked him if he could loan us the $180, which he graciously granted, and thus we paid off my dad and secured the title.

Now, for the past several months we had been making small payments to my uncle on *that* loan, but our cash flow came to a screeching halt with the inception of the 100% system. We did not believe the "house" needed to know about or take on this personal loan, so we figured we would just have to eke out my uncle's balance gradually, from our allowances.

Then an opportunity presented itself. This uncle and aunt owned some rental properties and one day she mentioned she was going refrigerator shopping, for one of their units. I told her we owned a working refrigerator, not in use, in the dining room at Beth Israel. I asked her if perhaps we could give it to them in lieu of the $80 we still owed. This proved agreeable to all parties so, one fine day, the Coppertone monster was hauled away and our debt was cleared.

On Saturday mornings, everyone lined up like obedient children to receive their allowance. Our allotment was $5 each for Don and me, and $2 each for Bethany and Benjamin. Reluctantly, it seemed, Jon handed us $14 in return for Don's paycheck. In our case it was like a reverse tithe—the house kept the 90%, and 10% was returned to us.

Don and I began a tradition of taking a walk to Baskin & Robbins for ice cream cones on Sunday afternoons, now that the weather was warming up. After lunch, we would put the kids down for naps, engage one of the sisters to baby-sit, and set out on our anticipated date. "B an' R," as we called it, was about three-quarters of a mile away, on Burnside, just before it began climbing into the west hills. A single-dip sugar cone cost 75 cents, a small fortune for us.

Once in a blue moon, we splurged on a snack at Rose's Delicatessen, a northwest Portland landmark famous for its seven-layer cakes, or went to the more modest Quality Pie Shop on 23rd. By carefully budgeting, we squeezed every drop out of our allowance, making it reach for gifts, clothing, personal toiletries, disposable diapers, postage, camera film and developing, not to mention gas and upkeep for our car.

One Saturday morning, a young man knocked on our door inquiring if Don's bike was for sale. He must have really wanted Ole Brown because he offered to pay $25 for it. Don turned him down though, explaining that he needed the bike to get to work and that it wasn't worth it to him to sell it.

When we came home from church the next day, Ole Brown was gone. The chain had been cut and was hanging limply from the porch railing, swaying in the breeze. We could not believe our eyes! Perhaps the guy who had asked to buy it wanted it so badly that he had stolen it when no one was home. Or maybe it was coincidental; it could have been anyone.

Don was depressed following his loss, for in addition to being victimized, he now had no choice but to drive to work, incurring more expense and inconvenience for us.

Kathy moved out about this time, so I decided to take over cutting all the brothers' hair in her stead. I had been cutting Don's hair ever since we got married and had become fairly good at it. If I could cut Don's super-straight, silky-fine hair, I was confident I could cut anyone's.

I didn't charge for the service, per se, but usually a brother would give me a dollar or two, which I welcomed as a little more spending money. We had recently added two new guys to the house, so my haircut clientele numbered an average of six.

The new guys, Klaus and Wayne, were housed in the attic. Klaus was an amiable young German man with dark curly hair and a brisk gait. He drove a neon-green Volkswagen Beetle and was quite helpful and polite around the house. He was fond of our children, often talking and playing with them. But after he repeatedly commented that our Bethany was going to be a "knockout" when she grew up and that she possessed "finesse," I began to fear he was developing an unnatural affinity for her. I never let her out of my sight when he was around.

Wayne was quite a bit older than the rest of us, probably in his late-30s. He was tall and lanky, kind of a cowboy type. He owned a guitar and was always sitting around playing it. He made no secret of his aspiration to become another Kris Kristofferson. In fact, he did look a lot like Mr. Kristofferson and, he made it clear to us, he also hoped he sounded like him. He continually asked the house-mates if we thought he sang good enough to make it in Nashville. His sullen personality was expressed in his melancholy music; he often sang Kristofferson's *Why Me, Lord?*, which was a popular hit at the time.

Finally, in early May, Willard showed up at church to make his public confession. His loyal, courageous wife accompanied him to the podium. He wept as he recounted his fall into temptation and immorality. He begged the congregation to forgive him and uphold him with prayerful support as he and his wife went on to another church in search of healing and restoration.

Apparently the revelation had remained a well-kept secret, as the congregation was at first stunned, then reduced to weeping and praying. Chuck asked the congregants to say in unison, "We forgive you, brother," as Willard walked down the aisle toward the door, his wife on his arm. Many clasped his hand or hugged him as he passed. Not an eye was dry.

Unfortunately, Willard's confession opened up an ugly can of worms. The remainder of the service was unexpectedly consumed by brothers and sisters coming forward to confess their sins of immorality, too. This pattern continued for several weeks, almost to the point of redundancy. It was way too much information and we all began to be suspect of one another.

The night before we left for California, the housemates wished us well around the dinner table. Jay presented us with a little picture he had made; imprinted on leather from Noah's Ark was a likeness of our family motoring down Interstate-5.

We were excited to be going on vacation. We really needed a change of scenery. It would be refreshing to get away from the house and the church for a bit, away from its oppressive cycle of sin and confession.

Once we arrived, however, it appeared we were merely getting out of the frying pan and into the fire. Returning to my parents' home as a guest—with my husband and children in tow—was always stressful for me. There was the big build-up of "glad to see you again," which rapidly deflated into the damp, shrunken balloon of frayed nerves and hot-button topics.

My sisters, Jane, 18, and Joyce, 16, gave up their bedroom for us. Since this visit was for my brother's wedding, thankfully my parents' home was not the frantic scene of the parents of the bride, but supposedly that of the calmer parents of the groom. Nevertheless, I vigilantly watched over our two-and-a-half year-old and nine month-old, to keep them out of trouble. I knew if I dared drop my guard there'd be heck to pay, in the form of my dad's gruff scolding and my mom's incessant chatter.

It felt strange returning for a wedding at the very church in which we had been married only three years earlier, especially since we were no longer members. Dale and Laurie's wedding was nice but of the typical Apostolic Christian Church variety—or should I say lack of variety—similar to our own. But it was encouraging to touch base again with many of my cousins and our old friends.

We made it to Disneyland the next day. Bethany loved the rides and looked cute wearing her muti-colored, "granny-square" sweater I had crocheted. She was thrilled to meet Mickey Mouse.

Later in the week, we drove down to the San Diego area to see Don's mom and sister, taking them with us on an outing to Palomar Observatory. We shared a picnic lunch and learned about the solar system. During our tour, when he tired of carrying the baby, Don set Benjie on the floor in front of an exhibit. Grabbing a pole, Benjie pulled himself up into standing position and then, while wagging his right index finger at the crowd, he began to jabber—"preaching" just like he had seen his Daddy doing. Don beamed as Benjie drew a crowd of amused onlookers.

When we spent the evening at Don's sister's house, we felt as though we had just dropped in from another planet. I guess we had totally forgotten how "regular people" lived. Our brother-in-law grilled an abundance of thick, juicy steaks, with so much left over that I found myself tallying how many soups and casseroles I could create out of them for the house. The beers flowed abundantly, though we didn't imbibe.

Donna mentioned to me that she had just bought groceries that day, spending $150 a week—half of it on meat—for her family of three! I reeled in shock and could not even bring myself to mention my food budget. She spent as much on groceries as my husband earned in total, and now he gave it all to the house. She knew we lived in a "commune," but I'm sure had no concept of what that meant. Since she portrayed no curiosity about it either, I decided not to offer any information.

The television blared all evening whether anyone was watching it or not. We caught glimpses of shows we had never even heard of, with titles like *Baretta* and *Starsky and Hutch*. It seemed like we lived in a parallel universe to the one on TV— the one of disco dancing, hot-pants and braless starlets.

Unable to spend the night there, as they had a small house and no extra beds, we retraced our two-hour drive back to my parents' home late that night.

As I washed the breakfast dishes the next morning, my mom asked me about the Prince of Peace. "Is it fundamental?" was her query. That was her way of implying that she hoped we hadn't fallen off the deep end.

I assured her that the people there were very plain—even to a fault—and humble-looking, with most of the women wearing ankle-length, homemade or hand-me-down skirts and covering their hair with bandanas. Also, I pointed out that the women were very "natural," without makeup or much jewelry. She was placated.

Later, my sister, Joyce, asked me why I didn't just tell Mom the truth—that it was a church full of hippies. "I know what it's *really* like," Joyce informed me. "I've heard all about it." She was referring to her correspondence with a Portland cousin of her own age, who didn't go to the Prince of Peace herself, but kept abreast of the action through her older sister and cousins.

But I believed I knew the best way to handle my mom. She certainly did not need to know the gory details about things in our life that she couldn't comprehend.

Of course, we also said nothing about the Willard issue, the current pastoral changeover, or the "100% system."

Even without this knowledge, my dad did not think highly of the Prince of Peace, so we certainly didn't need to make matters worse. He told me that he believed the POP leadership was attempting to keep everyone in poverty. In my naiveté, I disagreed.

CHAPTER SEVEN

ONSLAUGHT

Arriving home, we leaped right back onto the moving train that was Beth Israel. We were caught off-guard by the escalated pace which now propelled the house, as summer approached.

Jake and Monica had moved out. They found a little house to rent just across the river, in the southeast district. It was near enough to the cardboard box factory where Jake worked that he could walk, as they did not own a car.

Their former room was now occupied by two new girls, Sue and Pam, who had just finished their spring semester at Portland State and needed a place to live for the summer. Both seemed like nice Christian girls, quiet but helpful; they offered to baby-sit and willingly took their turns at cooking and household chores, which is what mattered to me.

Klaus was still living there, so we assumed he had become a Christian, since his allotted grace period would've definitely expired while we were gone. He had not been able to find a job yet, so he willingly accompanied the brothers to Noah's Ark each day, as did Wayne. Klaus was looking for a job in the meantime. Wayne was looking to go to Nashville.

Neighborhood people began stopping by for dinner, hanging out in the evening, and showing up for our Wednesday night Bible studies, which were open to the public. We continued holding our private house meeting/Bible study every Tuesday night.

That Wednesday evening, a neighborhood girl walked her immense Russian wolfhound over to the house and tied him up on our porch. Many of us went out to look at him, as he was the biggest dog we had ever seen. His back was waist high on Don and his head came up to Don's neck. I was not curious enough to risk finding out where he reached on me.

I let Bethany stay up during the Bible study that night, as she had napped in the afternoon. She was sitting on the couch beside me, in front of the picture window. Presently she got restless and stood up on the couch cushion, pressing her little face against the window glass. The dog, which had been lying on the porch, suddenly sprang up to his full height. He pushed his enormous, shaggy, gray head against the window, right in Bethany's face.

She let out a blood-curdling scream, turned pale and clung to me, terrified, shrieking and kicking hysterically. I tried to comfort her by taking her from the room and explaining that it was only a dog and it was outside and couldn't get her. This interruption broke up the study, as the girl who owned the dog apologized and left.

Several of Bethany's favorite housemates even tried to calm her down, but nothing worked. It took a long time to get her subdued enough to fall asleep that night, for she literally had been scared half to death.

By ten months old, Benjie had not quite mastered the art of climbing out of his crib, but Bethany took the initiative of climbing in and joining him. One afternoon, when they should have been sleeping, I peeked in only to find them both in the crib, and the baby looked like he had been tarred and feathered!

Bethany had taken the jar of Vaseline and the Johnson's Baby Powder (both were the enormous, economy size) from the changing table shelf and into his crib with her. There she began implementing her premeditated plans for Benjie.

First she slathered every nano-inch of the baby's clothed body with an impenetrably thick layer of petroleum jelly. Her next step was to dump the entire canister of powder all over him, coating him from head to toe.

"What are you doing?!" I exploded as I walked into the room, viewing the disaster.

"I'm powdering Baby Benny," was her meek reply. There he sat, the greased pig, completely caked in white, gasping for air.

Words fail my attempt to describe how difficult it was to remove thirty-six ounces *each* of Vaseline and baby powder from an infant, a toddler, their clothing, crib, walls and floor.

Not to be deterred from her goal of being mother's little helper, yet another day I found Bethany in his crib, this time "changing Baby Benny." She had completely undressed him, even removing his poopy diaper. Next, they had smeared the poop all over each other. I arrived in time to catch them in the act of finger painting the poop onto the crib sides and wallpapered walls, amidst a flux of hysterical giggles.

After screaming and gasping for air, I opened the windows to rid the room of the horrid stench. Then I removed the children to the bathroom and proceeded to hose them down in the shower. After thoroughly scrubbing, drying and redressing them, I set them both down on Bethany's bed, warning them not to move.

They watched sheepishly as I tackled the disgusting poop-fest, first removing the bedding and toys, then scrubbing down the crib, the mattress and lastly the walls. Thus far in my life, an occasion had not arisen requiring me to wash poop off walls.

The extent of this mess was unbelievable and it took me the remainder of the afternoon to clean it up. Thank goodness it was not my turn to make dinner that day, or I would've had to bail. The fetidness lingered on the second floor for days. Needless to say, I decided Bethany had outgrown her "afternoon nap" once and for all.

With two naughty little children and a house teaming with needy people, it began to dawn on me that I was not going to have time to plant a vegetable garden in the backyard.

Obviously, I was falling far short of being the perfect Proverbs 31 woman, who "purchased a field and planted it, and brought forth produce," and this really bothered me. The yard was overgrown with weeds; we had no money to rent a rotor-tiller and, besides, how was I going to eke out money for garden seeds from my dismal grocery budget? Don was swamped with leading Bible studies and doing counseling, and I certainly didn't have time to go outside with a shovel and turn over a garden patch.

Adding insult to injury, I spoke with a favorite cousin of mine on the phone, who—even though she, too, lived in one of the communal houses—had managed to plant a lovely, thriving garden. She advised me to *make* the time to do the same. She educated me on the upcoming berry seasons, stating that she would be picking the various berries at their proper times, freezing some and making jam for her house.

I explained why I was unable to do a garden, but admitted I might like to pick strawberries, as their season was almost upon us. I reminded her that she didn't have nearly as many people living at her house as I did.

"We're so crowded here that we have brothers rooming in the attic in sleeping bags," I divulged. No sooner had the words left my mouth than I realized mentioning this was a terrible mistake.

"Sleeping bags?" she chided, with exaggerated astonishment. "*Our* brothers have beds. I would *never* allow anyone to sleep in sleeping bags. Sleeping bags are for camping, not for houses!"

"Well, these brothers don't have beds and we aren't going to turn them away because of that," I attempted, in a feeble defense of myself and them.

And that night, true to form, we added another brother to the attic mix. This one, at least, was a stable Christian. His name was Dan and he came to us for the purpose of "training" in preparation for going into the mission field.

There was only one problem, he brought his dog. It was an ugly, scroungy mutt named Chopper, so similar in looks and temperament to Toto on *The Wizard of Oz*, that it must have been his evil twin. Dan knew we had a "no-pets" rule, but apparently he was above the law, for though many of us objected, Chopper moved in, too.

Unfortunately for Don and me, Dan and Chopper bedded down on the attic floor right above our bedroom. At night we could hear the annoying clickety-click of the dog's paws as he paced the floor, walking in circles before lying down, then rolled and fidgeted trying to get settled.

He was a hyper, jumpy little animal, a complete nuisance around the house. I was constantly chasing Chopper out of the kitchen—as were the other sisters—especially when we were trying to cook. Dan just thought it was amusing and made up a little ditty to further antagonize us.

"Poor little Chopper," he would chant. "Chopper runs into the kitchen. Sisters scream 'Ah! Ah!' Chopper runs out of the kitchen. Poor little Chopper." He would keep repeating this until satiated.

If Dan hadn't been such a good friend of Chuck and Mary's, and a member of their band, we probably would have ousted him. As it was though, I decided to grin and bear it, for in spite of the Chopper issue, Dan was a solid brother and we needed his good influence in the house.

At this point, house morale truly hit an all-time low. Admittedly, both Don and I were discontent following our trip to California. I was overwhelmed with cooking and housework without Monica there to share the load. All the other sisters were single and had jobs. I began feeling like I was married to a dozen unappreciative slobs.

Bickering developed between the sisters regarding house-keeping chores, room furnishings and privacy issues; between the brothers over doctrinal differences, workplace issues and unspoken grudges. Attendance at the mandatory prayer meetings and Bible studies became sporadic. Maybe it was spring fever, or the 100% system was taking its toll; I don't know. Whatever the reasons, Don was constantly counseling people and mediating disputes, and I was forever picking up the slack.

On Friday, when Jon gave me the grocery money, he seemed so aloof that it made me too uncomfortable to try and wrestle extra money from him for my berry-picking plans. My innate shyness overtook me so, when Don got home from work, I asked him to talk to Jon about my idea of picking strawberries to make jam for the house.

Don did so, later, and managed to squeeze $10 out of him for our berry-picking adventure. I drove to Fred Meyer's that night and got the majority of the grocery shopping done, thus freeing up the next morning for our outing.

Saturday morning I felt exhilarated as our little family headed out of the city towards the lush farmlands of Sauvie Island. My heart swelled with inspiration as we followed the lovely banks of the Willamette River—rolling calmly along, its eventual destination the sea. "Oh, if only we could live in the country," I sighed, wistfully, as we crossed the bridge onto the island. Don nodded.

Placing Benjie in his stroller—with a bottle of juice, crackers and several toys—we meandered our way through the field to our assigned rows. Bethany "helped" us fill our containers, though she ate more than she bucketed. I picked fast, knowing that due to the kids being with us, our time was sorely limited.

About forty-five minutes into it, I indicated to Don that we should wrap it up, brilliantly basing my deduction on the evidence at hand: Benjie's emptied bottle, toys and crackers lying in the mud, and a stream of diarrhea oozing down his pant legs; Bethany's berry-stained face, hands and shirt, and a puddle of magenta-colored vomit swirling at her feet.

We transported our treasured strawberries—and our filthy kids—homeward, thrilling to the deep red color and the delicious fragrance permeating the car.

Back at the house, we voiced our intentions for the berries, warning everyone not to eat them. Since I had just done the grocery shopping the night before, the refrigerator and freezer were full. We sure could've used that spare refrigerator right about now, I regretted, but it was long gone. I decided to store the berries in the basement overnight, where it was much cooler, hoping they would keep better.

Sunday morning at breakfast, I told everyone why the berries were being stored in the basement, and of their purpose, reminding them not to eat any. The basement dwellers had already eaten quite a few, but weren't fessing up to it. I should have known not to leave food down there to tempt those starving guys.

After church, while the sisters babysat, Don and I went on our usual walk, but this time our destination was Fred Meyer's instead of Baskin Robbins. Finding the home-canning aisle, I desperately looked for any clues on how to make freezer jam, for the last thing I wanted to do was ask my cousin. I was stunned to realize I needed to buy several boxes of pectin, tons of white sugar and dozens of plastic pint-size containers.

The $10 we had received from Jon was but a drop in the bucket. The berries alone had already cost over $12; the balance we had paid with our own money. Now the supplies to make jam were going to be at least that much again. But it was too late now; we were into this operation too deeply, so we paid for the additional trappings with our precious allowance.

Upon arriving home, there wasn't time to tackle my berry project. Don couldn't help me, as he rushed off to meet Ron, Nick and a few other brothers in front of the downtown stadium—joining them to preach to the crowds as the ball game let out.

After giving the kids their dinner and getting them ready for bed, I finally made it down to the basement to check on my berries. I grumbled as I discovered the levels were down considerably lower than what we had picked, but no one was home to scold. It was such an unseasonably hot weekend that many of my beauties had spoiled.

It took me four trips to the basement to carry all the containers upstairs, alone. Feeling my anger and anxiety rise, I sped through the process of trimming or tossing the moldy ones, while my kids sat on the kitchen floor in their pajamas, playing with pots and pans. Finding three cookie sheets, I washed and hulled the nicest berries, placing them on the sheets to freeze whole.

As the housemates began trickling home, they wandered into the kitchen and started bugging me with questions about what I was doing—all the while popping berries into their mouths. I had two cookie sheets full of berries on top of the stove, one tray perched on top of the garbage can, berries in both sinks and berries piled on the counters in various stages of preparation. Additionally, I had open bags of sugar, boxes of pectin, measuring cups and bowls set out. Catching a glimpse of the clock, I suddenly realized it was after 8, and time to put my whiny kids to bed.

"Stay out of the strawberries!" I reprimanded everyone within ear-shot. "I have plans for them." I took the kids upstairs, having no choice but to leave my project unattended.

While I was nursing the baby in the red chair, Don came upstairs, home from preaching. Glancing up at him, I immediately noticed something was wrong, as he wore a mortified expression on his face. His hair and military fatigue-jacket were matted with bits of a brown and white, greasy substance. "What happened?" I quizzed.

"I got hit in the face with a pie," he answered seriously, then chuckled, trying to abate the impact of the assault.

I couldn't quite believe him. "You're kidding!" I stared at his face for a clue.

"No, really," he grimaced. "It was a chocolate cream pie and, you know, I don't even like chocolate!" His voice escalated and he stuck out his tongue, indicating his distaste and still attempting to lighten the seriousness of the situation. He laughed, adding, "At least it could've been my favorite, coconut cream."

Realizing it was true, I was overwhelmed by a surge of pride, compassion and fear for my brave, humiliated husband. His face maintained a pallid, chagrined look as he removed his outer garments and tossed them into the hamper behind the door. I could tell he didn't want to talk about it, for he headed straight into the bathroom to shower.

I was dumbfounded. Though we were aware there was an element of danger involved when he went street preaching, nothing had ever happened to him before. The fact that he was hit with a pie made the incident amusing, but the fact that he was hit *at all* gave it a serious tone. It could have been a fist or a weapon. We both were more sobered by the event than we dared to admit.

I carefully laid our sleeping son in his crib, kissed and tucked in our drowsy daughter, and softly closed their door. I heard the shower water running in the bathroom so, leaving my family upstairs, I put on my brave face and trotted downstairs to re-tackle my strawberries.

Most of the housemates were home now and were mulling around in the kitchen, making tea and delving into their private stashes for Sunday night snacks. It looked like they had left my project alone.

Ted was sitting on the counter holding a mug of steaming tea. "I heard about what happened to Don," he said. "Is he okay?" He sounded genuinely concerned.

"Well, yeah," I downplayed, casually. "It was just a pie." Apparently they not only knew about the incident, but seemed amused by it—tittering a bit as I entered the room. My hands began trembling and I wasn't sure why. "It's not funny, you know," I added, my voice taking on an unbecoming testiness. "It could've been something worse. He might've been hurt!"

Dan ambled into the kitchen, Chopper at his heels. The dog's paws annoyingly clicked on the floor as he paced, while his owner stood at the stove. "Chopper, get out!" I ordered, but the dog looked at Dan and chose to disobey me.

"Can all of you *please* leave the kitchen?" I quivered. "I've got all these berries to work on and they're starting to go bad!"

My anxiety level was piquing, my eyes were tearing up and I knew I'd better get a grip. I tried to ignore them as they shuffled around the kitchen, gathering up their snacks.

Suddenly I wished I could be anywhere else right now instead of in this stupid house with these stupid people! So this is what I get for totally surrendering my life to you, God! I get stuck serving these unappreciative, immature babies while my husband gets assaulted on the street corner for spreading your Word! I had had it with God, and was so upset that I couldn't see straight.

"Can I help?" a male voice offered, but I didn't make eye contact with the speaker.

"No," I countered, and then quavered, "I just need to be left alone so I can concentrate."

That must have been Jay, I thought, as I caught a glimpse of him leaving the room. Ignoring the others that were lingering, I got out the largest saucepan and measured sugar and pectin into it. As I held the colander full of berries under the running water at the sink, Chopper ran back into the kitchen. That was the last straw.

"Will someone please get this dog out of here?" I hollered, but it was too late.

Chopper stood up on his hind legs, placing his paws on the cookie sheet full of berries, which was balanced precariously on the garbage can. The tray clattered to the floor, sending strawberries flying in all directions. A second later, the startled dog—clambering to keep his balance—upset the brimming garbage can, spewing its contents all over the floor and onto my precious berries.

I screamed, dropping the sieve into the sink. As people ran back into the kitchen, coming from both directions—squashing tea grounds, plate scrapings and strawberries underfoot—I totally freaked out.

"I can't take this anymore!" I shrieked, bolting from the kitchen. Darting through the foyer, I caught sight of Don strolling down the stairs, combing his clean, wet hair, oblivious to the drama. I swung the front door open wide and ran blindly down the stoop and into the street.

Adrenaline-soaked, I turned and ran up Hoyt Street—my heart pounding, about to burst from my chest. I don't care what happens anymore, I panted. I'm sick of this house and all this responsibility. I can't do this. I want to crack up. I want to get away. Just let me go, God, let me fall apart! I was totally discombobulated, the tension pulling so tightly within me that I was sure my final thread of sanity was going to snap.

When I reached 23rd, I leaped onto the sidewalk to avoid traffic, turned right and slowed my pace. I suddenly realized that it was dark, and late; it must have been after 9. I heard my name being called and turned to see Don approaching.

"What are you doing? Where are you going?" he asked, wrapping a comforting arm around my shoulder.

Sobbing spasmodically, I poured out my heart, begging him to save me from this crazy house. Turning at the next corner, we walked slowly around the block. By the time we approached the house, I had regained most of my composure. Darn it! I fumed. God won't even let me fall apart when I want to!

"I'm not going back in there," I pouted, pausing on the stoop. "I don't want anyone to see me and I don't *ever* want to see that kitchen again. Just go throw the whole mess away."

"It's okay," Don soothed, "you don't have to see anyone. Go on up to our room and I'll clean up the kitchen."

As we hurried inside, we heard voices coming from behind the closed kitchen door. I zipped up the stairs, thankfully avoiding any people. I checked on the kids, who were sound asleep, then changed into my nightgown and got into bed. Then I broke down crying again, pounding my pillow, tossing and turning. I wanted my privacy. I wanted my life back. And I didn't care anymore how selfish and evil that meant I was.

Don was gone a long time and I heard several others come upstairs—opening and closing doors, and using the bathrooms—before he appeared. Finally he came into our room and sat on the edge of the bed. "You're not going to believe it," he whispered. "They all pitched in, cleaned up everything and finished working on your berries."

"Working on?" I sniveled. I could only imagine what *that* might mean.

"Yeah, they washed and sorted them for you and threw away the bad ones. They even emptied the garbage and mopped the floor. The berries are in the refrigerator so you can make the jam tomorrow while everyone's at work."

"Yeah, right," I muttered to my pillow as I turned my face away from Don. "We'll see."

He stood up, adding, "I need to go talk to Klaus about something. Be right back."

Typical, I seethed. There was always someone or something more important than us.

Next morning, I was pleased to find the kitchen showed no sign of last night's crisis. I was also very grateful no one mentioned the incident, as I felt ashamed of myself for making such a big scene. But maybe we all had learned something from this: I certainly was not perfect and self-sufficient—their kitchen steward had a breaking point, too— and that teamwork can't hurt.

At the breakfast table, Klaus suprised us by announcing his farewell. With his distinctive flourish and expressing appreciation to us all, he stood and bowed deeply, kissed his fingertips, waved his hand and bid us *adieu*.

Awhile later, as the last housemate was leaving for work, he came into the nook where I was feeding the kids, kissed them each goodbye and gave me a big hug. "I think very highly of your family," he confided, "and I wish you all a good life. I didn't mean you any harm."

I didn't quite know what he meant by that, but I watched him hoist his army-drab knapsack over his shoulder and saunter out the door. I followed, locking the door behind him, then peered through the window and waved as he got into his Beetle and drove away.

Enjoying Monday morning's serenity, I nimbly tackled my strawberry projects. First I filled eight containers with the best whole berries. I crushed all that remained with the potato masher, cooked them in the sugar and pectin, and then filled ten pint containers with freezer jam. After doing a little shuffling, I managed to fit them all snuggly into the freezer.

In the end, I netted less than one-third of my potential product, having lost the balance to nibbling and waste. Well at least that's done, I sighed, shutting the freezer door with finality.

That night, Don updated me on the Klaus story. Apparently dormmate Dan had observed Klaus dabbling in the black arts in the attic, and told Don of his concerns. Klaus had been caught holding séances, inviting spirits into the house and had practiced spells on house members by use of tarot cards. He revealed that he was a student of the writings of Edgar Cayce.

As Don cautiously counseled Klaus about knowing God by means of a relationship with Christ, according to the Bible, Klaus opened his Cayce books and read portions to Don. He insisted he was following the same God, just reaching Him in a different manner, and that there was no harm in what he was doing.

Don pointed out that "divination" was an attempt to manipulate or control our lives and environment, while Christianity was a lifestyle based on a growing relationship with God, by following Jesus Christ and His teachings. Don told Klaus that he could relate to his propensity, however, for he too had been drawn to the black arts before becoming a Christian, but now recognized the danger in it.

After a lengthy discussion, Klaus refused to waver. Don concluded by presenting him with the bottom line: These practices were not in agreement with the beliefs and goals of Beth Israel and he would have to cease doing them or leave. Unfortunately, even though their talk had been positive and non-confrontational, Klaus agreed to move out rather than change.

Tuesday morning, still discomfited from the events of the last few days, I busied myself in the kitchen as everyone left for work. Hearing no sound yet from my children's bedroom above me, I buttered a piece of toast and sat down at the nook table to eat it with my second cup of tea. I loved this time of day, after everyone had gone to work and the house was silent. I could relax and make believe it was my own home.

It was a dreary, drizzly morning. I gazed wistfully out the window at the colorless, leaden sky. It's still so dark out, I thought. That must be why the kids are sleeping in. I wished I could go back to bed, too. Maybe I could, I pondered, as I was still in my usual early morning attire of nightgown and light green quilted robe.

Suddenly, I heard a door handle click and I turned, startled, to see Wayne step out of the small bathroom in the hallway. "What are you doing here?" I asked, trying to sound calm. Had he purposely been waiting in there all this time, until everyone else was gone and I was alone?

"It's 8:30," I said sharply, glancing at the clock. I stood to my feet as he approached. He was staring at me strangely.

"I'm leavin' today," he drawled. "Goin' to Nashville."

"Well, you need to leave *now*. You shouldn't be here. No one's supposed to be in the house after eight o'clock," I reminded him. He was standing too close.

I stepped back against the table, resting my left hand on its surface to steady myself. "Do the guys know you're here?" I asked, hoping he couldn't sense the fear in my voice.

He continued staring directly into my face, making me very uncomfortable. "I want you to come with me," he murmured gently. "When you cut my hair the other night, I realized I was in love with you."

This can't be happening! I thought. Trembling, my eyes darted around the room, my gaze resting on the bread, butter and butter knife still out on the counter by the sink.

"No," I said firmly, "I'm not going with you. I'm happily married. You need to leave right now!" I slipped past him and walked over to the counter. "Do you want some toast to take with you?" I asked, hoping to distract him. I inserted two slices of bread into the toaster.

He sauntered over and stood behind me. "I don't think you're married at all," he suggested slyly. "You don't even have a wedding ring."

"I *am* married and I love my husband very much," I refuted his accusation with a quivering voice. I have to get out of this house, I thought, but the kids are upstairs. I can't just run out of the house for help, leaving them in here alone. My mind was racing.

"Here, have some tea," I offered, pouring him a cup. I carried it back to the nook and set it on the table, hoping he would follow, and I could dash out of the room. He didn't.

Suddenly the toast popped up and we both jumped, jerking our heads to stare at it. I walked deliberately towards it.

"I'm getting a recording contract in Nashville," he was saying. "I could give you a better life than this. Don isn't worthy of you. You deserve better and I'd give it to you." His words were flowing smoothly now, as he drew up his courage.

"No!" I spoke louder. "You need to go!" I frantically buttered the toast and reached for a plate to put it on, as he slid up behind me. He raised his right hand and touched my hair. "Don't do that!" I demanded, brushing his arm away. "Here, have some toast. I don't think you ate breakfast." I walked back to the table and placed it near the tea, motioning for him to come and sit down. He ambled back over to the table and stood staring at me.

Sit down! My mind screamed. I brushed past him, returning to the counter again. Intentionally I closed the bread bag with a twisty-tie and placed the lid on the butter container, all the while watching him out of the corner of my eye.

He slowly pulled out a chair and, as he began to sit, he took his eyes off me for just a moment. In that split second, I cautiously insinuated myself between the butter knife and his gaze, then quickly slipped the knife into the deeply recessed left pocket of my robe.

He looked up at me again and I hoped he hadn't noticed that move. I had no idea what I was going to do with a butter knife, and I desperately prayed I would not have to find out.

"Come with me," he coaxed again.

"No!" I repeated. "You need to leave as soon as you've eaten." Then in an instant, I made my move to the doorway, kicked up the doorstop, and exited the kitchen. The swinging door closed behind me, creating a buffer between us. Darting into the foyer, I grabbed the phone and quickly dialed Noah's Ark by rote.

Jon answered. "This is Judy," I panted, little more than whispering. "Wayne is in the house, and I'm scared of him. Come home immediately!" Just as I set the receiver back on the cradle, my hand still hovering over it, Wayne appeared in the hallway. Maybe he thinks I'm just now picking it up, I hoped. Maybe he didn't hear me talking, I prayed.

"Oh, come on, now. You don't have to call anyone," he purred, in his Southern accent. "I'm not goin' to hurt you."

"You need to leave *right now!*" I yelled at him, pointing to the door with all the severity I could muster. "And I need to take care of my kids." Crossing his path, I started up the stairs, praying under my breath in the unknown tongues of duress. Oh God! I thought. Protect us. I don't know what to do.

He followed me right up the stairway, just two steps behind. "Don't come upstairs!" I ordered. "You need to leave *now!*"

"Come with me," he cajoled, grabbing at the fabric of my right sleeve. "I love you."

I shook my arm free of his hand. "No! Don't touch me! You need to leave!" I ran up the remaining steps, hearing his breath at the back of my neck. Pray, pray, pray, was all I could do. Oh God help me!! My mind whirled in terror. I don't know what to do!

He was right on my heels as I crossed the landing, opened the kids' bedroom door and slammed it shut behind me. I stood with my back against the door to hold it closed. The kids were both awake and looked up at me. Benjie began jumping and laughing in his crib.

"Good morning, dollies," I feigned a smile at them, trying to sound like nothing was wrong. I didn't move a muscle, expecting Wayne to push the door open at any moment.

My eyes darted around the room as I narrowed my choices. Could we survive jumping from a second-floor window to escape Wayne? I fingered the butter knife in my pocket. There was nothing separating us from him except a one-inch-thick piece of wooden door.

But the door didn't open.

I continued standing there, my back against the door, for what seemed an eternity. I heard no sound—no breathing, no movement, no voice, no footsteps. He must be standing as still as I am, right on the other side of the door, I thought. He's waiting for me to open it when I think he's gone. I didn't budge.

Suddenly, a male voice hollered up from the foyer, "Hello! Hello, Judy! Anybody here?" I heard feet taking the stairs two at a time as the voice got closer. "Hello, Judy! It's Jay!"

I opened the door cautiously. "Did you see him?" I gushed, so relieved to see Jay that I almost collapsed. "Did you pass him on the stairs?"

Jay was about to collapse, himself, having run the seven blocks from Noah's Ark in a few short minutes. "No," he panted, "I didn't see anyone."

"He was trying to get me to go with him. He followed me up the stairs. He was right outside this door," I explained, shaking like a leaf. I stood clinging to the doorway while Jay searched each of the second floor rooms and closets.

"I'll check the attic," Jay offered. Momentarily, he came back down. "No one's up there," he said, lighting from the bottom step.

I couldn't imagine where Wayne had gone, as only moments earlier he was inches away from me. "I didn't hear him walk away from the door," I told Jay. "It's almost like he disappeared."

Jay offered to stay and search the whole house while I hurriedly dressed and got the kids changed. Presently, I brought them downstairs and joined Jay in the nook. The tea and toast I had desperately extended to Wayne remained untouched on the table, a grim reminder. Shuddering, I quickly poured the tea down the drain and tossed the toast into the garbage, washing my hands of the horror.

I related to Jay how Wayne had been begging me to go to Nashville with him, and wouldn't take no for an answer. "He wouldn't leave, and he was following me and kept trying to touch me," I shivered. "Thank you, Jay, for getting home so fast." I gave him a hug. He was truly my hero.

"Wayne's gone now," he assured me, then added matter-of-factly, "I think God took him." I was astonished to hear him say that, for it was exactly what I had been thinking.

Jay lingered at the house for another half hour or so, seated at the table while I prepared and fed my kids their breakfast. He apologized excessively for the oversight he and the other brothers had exhibited, by not noticing that Wayne had remained in the house that morning. He maintained that he and the other leather shop guys should have missed Wayne not accompanying them to work, but somehow they had let it slip right by. Insisting on bearing the blame, he begged my forgiveness, which I bestowed.

As I talked with Jay, I found my nerves were calmed and I regained my composure. Admittedly apprehensive when he left to return to work, I locked the front door behind him and watched as he strolled down the stoop and headed towards 21st.

Immediately I went to the phone and dialed Reed Electric. Don worked on a production line and was not allowed to take phone calls, but I left a message for him to call me.

Shortly after 10, on his morning break, he returned my call and I relayed the incident to him. Don was quite unnerved by my rendition and insisted on coming home at noon, which he did. He checked and re-checked every room on all four floors—all the closets, doors and windows—and was reluctant to return to work at 12:25.

At dinner, the hot topic was the "Wayne incident," as it came to be known. Everybody put in their two-cents-worth on how it could have been avoided, and how I had handled it. None of us ever saw or heard from Wayne again.

Judy, Bethany and Benjamin on the front porch roof,
soaking up some long-awaited sunshine.

CHAPTER EIGHT

ADDICTIONS

A few weeks earlier, shortly before our trip to California, we had received our tax refund from the previous year, a tidy sum of $230. We were not required to give it to the house—as it was not considered "income" and was based on our finances pre-Beth Israel—so, after tithing on it, we deposited the remainder into our humble savings account. Then right before we left for California, we had withdrawn all our money to use for gas, lodging and entertainment on the trip.

Now we had about $50 remaining and Don adamantly maintained it was time we buy wedding rings, especially in the wake of the Wayne incident. Though having rings or not meant very little to us at the time, it apparently meant a great deal to the rest of the world in which we lived. So, after thoroughly discussing and praying about the issue for the next few days, we finally concluded that there was nothing sinful about wearing a band of gold on one's finger.

On Saturday, after arranging for the kids to be babysat at the house, we found ourselves wandering through jewelry stores in downtown Portland. We had no idea how much a simple gold band would cost. The first store proved quite pricey, so at the second one, we disclosed right up front how much we had to work with.

We were shown matching gold bands with an unobtrusive, diagonal etching engraved on them. They were $30 each and both our sizes were in stock. When we tried them on, they fit perfectly, so we decided not to belabor the process any further. Prudently, we counted out our $60, thankful that Oregon had no sales tax. With the allowance we had received that morning, we had exactly enough money for the rings and ice cream cones at B&R on our way home.

Around the dining table that evening, the housemates all expressed their delight as we showed off our rings. They congratulated us on finally being "legal."

It was remarkable what wearing a wedding ring did for my self-esteem. The next day I was full of ambition. I finished making my pink, crinkle-gauze summer dress, even taking the time to embroider pastel flowers on the front yoke and the cap-sleeve edges.

And since it wasn't my turn to cook dinner, I decided to cut my hair. I had read in a magazine article that the way to give yourself a perfectly layered haircut was to lean your head upside down, determine the desired length and then cut straight across.

I worked up my courage, took a deep breath and, brandishing a sharp pair of scissors, I leaned over and cut away. I swung my head back up and met my face in the mirror; now it was fringed by lightly feathered, bouncy layers. It looked cute, fresh and fun. In one quick snip I was liberated from my former, limited choices—the long ponytail or frumpy bun—which I had dutifully worn for several years. Now I was buoyant and free, looking—I hoped—just the slightest bit like one of *Charlie's Angels*!

When Don came home that evening I bounded down the stairs, surprising him with my new look. "I cut my hair!" I announced. "Do you like it?" My tone turned into a plea.

"Well, I guess I'm going to have to," was his banal reply.

Don always said he loved my long hair, but I didn't care. I liked my new shorter tresses and I needed it. I had lived so long on the opposing side of the emerging feminist movement, always striving to be the "godly woman" of I Timothy 2—even to the point of severity.

I allowed myself to question, for the first time really, if being so plain and grave actually pleased God more than just being normal. Was it actually an issue with Him, or merely based on people's traditions and expectations?

Next thing we knew, the Rose Festival season was upon us. This annual June event marks the blooming of roses all over town, especially at the Rose Test Gardens in the southwest hills. It is celebrated by a queen and her court, a riverfront carnival and a lavish downtown parade with floral floats.

Our house was assigned scheduled times to go out witnessing and passing out tracts at the events. We viewed every public gathering as a witnessing opportunity. I guess it never occurred to us that we could attend the festivities for fun and recreation like regular people.

Don went down to the carnival to preach several nights that week. On Saturday afternoon, the kids and I accompanied him. Baby Benjie "preached" from his stroller, and little Bethany helped pass out tracts like the grown-ups.

Every possible religious cult was represented in the surging throng. There were members of Holy Order of MANS outfitted in their flowing, white, biblical robes. Mormon elders rode by on bicycles, wearing their trademark white shirts which sharply contrasted with their black neckties and pants.

The colorful Hare Krishna—adorned with gauzy, orange sarongs and shaved heads—strutted in unison down the sidewalk, their bells jangling a merry rhythm: "chi-chi-chum, chi-chi-chi, chi-chi-chum, chi-chi." Pausing for a red light at the same corner we were standing on, they danced in place until the light turned green. As they crossed the street towards the carnival booths, a pretzel hawker capitalized on their approach by hollering out, "Hare! Hare! Step right up and get your hot, soft pretzels!" The crowd was amused.

That night, we added four new people—actually five—to our house; all had been invited back to Beth Israel from the Rose Festival. There was a girl named Bethlehem and her yet-unnamed newborn son, an attractive blond named Vanessa, and two Portland State University students: Kirk and another Don. The sisters made room for the female guests in their second-floor rooms, and the guys were relegated to the attic.

I took Bethlehem under my wing, talking "babies" with her at the kitchen nook table after the dinner dishes were done. She nursed her infant son discreetly as we shared experiences. She was 18, unmarried and homeless.

"I have some baby-boy clothes and blankets I'd like to give you, if you need them," I offered.

"Sure." She nodded, sounding grateful.

"Where were you living?" I probed, gently.

"I ran away from home almost a year ago," she admitted, "and never finished high school. I'm gonna see if my mom'll let me move home, now that...," she paused and looked down at the baby, "Well, you know..."

I was curious about her name. "Is your mom a Christian?" I prompted. "I mean, she named you Bethlehem, so I just wondered."

"My family went to church, but I quit going." She quickly changed the subject. "Who's that singing?" she asked, referring to the record that was playing in the dining room.

"Chuck Girard," I replied. "He's a really cool Christian singer." She silently twirled a lock of her shaggy, black hair in the fingers of her right hand.

I noticed her faded denim mini-skirt, rhinestone-trimmed, black T-shirt and shiny black boots. "I like your boots," I grinned, nodding in their direction.

"Thanks," she divulged a hint of a smile, then referring to the music again, added, "I like the band *Bad Company*."

At that very moment, Ted walked through the swinging door from the dining room to the nook and overheard her comment. "Bad company corrupts good morals," he quipped, interrupting us. "It says so in I Corinthians 15:33."

Bethlehem looked down self-consciously and turned away, suddenly aware that she was nursing with a man in the room. Ted ambled over to the sink and poured himself a tall glass of water. That figures, I thought. He's probably fasting again. Lately he would sit at the dinner table with us, but not eat, and was reducing himself to skin and bones. He exited the kitchen using the other door.

Bethlehem's countenance fell and her attitude altered drastically after that. "I need to put the baby to bed," she uttered, flatly, as she rose and left the room.

I was disturbed by Ted's rude intrusion, but I wasn't sure if I should tell him. She was just about to open up to me, I thought, and then he had to come in and ruin everything.

Later, I filled a bag with several receiving blankets and Benjie's outgrown sleepers and booties. I knocked gently on the door of the room she was sharing with Ann and Terry. She peered out cautiously, and then seeing it was me, opened the door wider.

"Here are some things you might be able to use for the baby," I whispered, as she took the bag.

"Thanks." She gave me the slightest hug and I was glad.

In the morning, she rode to church with Ann's car-load, and I noticed her sitting in a pew, rocking her sleeping son during the service. However, she did not reappear at the house after church. I questioned Terry as to Bethlehem's whereabouts.

"We didn't see her after church," Terry explained, "so we thought someone else took her home." Then quietly she confided, "I think she's a speed freak. She was up fidgeting around all night and didn't want to eat any breakfast. She knew she couldn't really stay here because she needs her fixes."

I realized I hadn't looked for Bethlehem at breakfast. I was too preoccupied getting my own family ready for church to check on her.

"I gave her a bag of baby clothes," I told Terry. "Can we look in your room and see if she took them?" Together we climbed the stairs and searched the room. The bag was not there, so I was relieved to know that she must have taken the things with her. I certainly hoped so, for she was going to need them.

"She must've walked away when church was over, right back into her downtown street-life," I shook my head, truly sorry.

Terry and I clasped hands and prayed for Bethlehem's protection and guidance. Maybe she would return to her mom and be accepted back but, if not, I trusted that God would lead her to another church or shelter for assistance.

Running a spiritual nursery was risky business; some make it to maturity and some fall through the cracks. There were no guarantees.

Vanessa was still with us Sunday evening and was quite a hit with the brothers. In her mid-20s, her face wasn't exactly pretty but her blond hair, good tan and nice figure more than compensated.

About eight of the single housemates went out to dinner at Rose's Deli that night. Don and I had put our kids to bed and were sitting in the parlor, reading and listening to records, when they returned. They were a rowdy group, talking and laughing loudly as they plopped down on the couch and floor. The guys all swarmed around Vanessa. As flirting and couch-pillow fights ensued, we took the hint and decided to go on up to our room.

Awhile later, just after we had gone to bed, there came a knock at our door. "Don! It's Jon," the voice pleaded. "We need your help downstairs." Don got up, pulled on his jeans and left the room. I put on my robe and followed him. As I turned the final tier on the stairway, I saw Vanessa lying on her back on the parlor floor, her body arching and flopping wildly, her eyes rolled back into her head. Don had joined Jon and Dan as they knelt around her.

"She's having a seizure," Dan looked up as I entered the room. "I'll try to grab her tongue so she doesn't swallow it." He deftly slipped two fingers into her mouth. She groaned and thrashed her arms about. Don attempted to secure her hands as he began praying over her, in the Spirit. Jon held onto her head to keep it from bouncing on the floor. Her hair and face were moist with a mix of sweat and drool. I kept my distance because I had no idea what to do.

After what seemed forever, she finally calmed down and her body lay still. They helped her to sit up, then stand and walk over to the couch, where she gingerly sat down. She glanced at me self-consciously. I knew she must be mortified to have people see her this way; her hair was matted and stringy, her chin dripping saliva. I went into the bathroom in the hallway and grabbed a towel, returning in time to hear her whisper, "I have epilepsy."

None of us knew what to say. Finally, Dan asked gently, "Do you take any medication for it?"

"Yes, usually, but I got prayed for at church today, so I don't need my meds anymore," she murmured.

"Well, maybe you haven't received your healing yet," Dan suggested, tactfully, "so it might be a good idea to keep taking them." She nodded.

"Do you want us to help you upstairs?" I offered.

"I'll take care of her," Jon quickly answered for Vanessa. With that, Dan, Chopper, Don and I climbed the stairs and dispersed to our respective rooms, leaving Jon and Vanessa seated on the couch.

The next morning, everyone congregated in the parlor at 6:30, as usual, for morning prayer. Jon was already sitting cross-legged on the floor, tuning his guitar, when we came downstairs.

About the time we began singing the second song, I woke up enough to notice that Vanessa wasn't in the circle, and the pocket doors to the dining room were slid wide open. I figured she must have left during the night. Who could blame her? After such a humiliating episode, I would, too.

But, boy was I wrong! Towards the end of our third song, the door of Jon's bedroom—the small room off the rear of the dining room—opened, and Vanessa emerged, clad only in a silky, pink, mini-length robe. She yawned and stretched, rubbing her eyes, then reached down to find the sash's loose strings and tie them around her waist to cover her nakedness.

Thank goodness most of the housemates hadn't seen her yet, as their eyes were closed in worship, but Don and I both did. We looked at each other quizzically, shook our heads and shrugged. I glanced up at her as she approached the parlor, and she gave me a dirty look, as if to say, "Mind your own business." She pulled up a chair from the dining table and sat down in the doorway, her bare, tan legs exposed all the way up.

I couldn't believe it!! Now Jon and Vanessa were sleeping together, and she was flaunting it, no less! What next? Man, she's got her nerve, I thought. If she thinks she can just sachet into a prayer meeting directly from our house-head's bedroom...

I was disgusted; I'd had about all of this I could stomach. Surely one of my children must need me, I thought. I have better things to do than to sit here with these people. I rose and exited the room, slipping quietly upstairs.

Later that evening, Don and I discussed what we should do with our knowledge of Jon and Vanessa. It was tempting to want to go to one of the co-pastors, tell him about the situation, and let him handle it.

Then we remembered the instructions of Jesus in Matthew 18. He said that if a brother has erred, you should go to him privately and discuss it, and only if he doesn't receive your admonition should you go to a third party.

That's always difficult to do, though. One's first tendency is to tell others instead of going directly to the person(s) involved. Don was reluctant to talk to Jon, as Jon was hard to approach about most anything—let alone this.

Several nights later, Don had an opportunity to speak to Jon privately. He told him that some of us were aware of his relationship with Vanessa, that it was inappropriate for the house and was affecting house morale. Jon assured Don that he understood where he was coming from, and that he had the situation under control.

He then disclosed to Don a secret we were not aware of— Vanessa had a drinking problem. He explained that he was covering for her by letting her stay in his room when she was drunk, as she was ashamed to go into the bedroom she was supposed to be sharing with Ann and Terry, lest she be discovered.

That next Saturday morning, our family drove to Fred Meyer's and bought a small green and yellow tricycle for Bethany. Don put it together on the porch, and then we showed her how to pedal it on the sidewalk. Summer was here and it was time to get outdoors.

We also bought several cans of motor oil and a filter. Our car was acting up, idling too high, and it desperately needed an oil change.

While we were out front, Kirk came onto the porch and when he noticed Don under the hood, he offered to help him. We were both relieved, as everyone knew Kirk was good at working on cars.

The guys discussed politics while I played with the kids. The topic *du jour* was the current state of affairs under President Ford's Republican regime, countered by the Democratic Party's platform for the upcoming November election. Kirk was a Political Science major and was all fired up about the current issues.

"You ought to read Karl Marx' *Communist Manifesto*," Kirk startled Don by saying. "I think you'd like what he has to say about the People's ongoing struggle against the Capitalists." Don was taken aback and tried to steer the conversation towards Christianity instead.

Later that afternoon, Kirk brought his slim, hard-cover, Marx volume up to our room, but Don turned down his offer to loan it to him, advising him to stick to the Bible.

It seemed like things were getting out of hand. The house was turning into a free-for-all and Don decided he'd had about enough. He went downstairs and found Jon, demanding that they call for a mandatory house meeting. But, in discussing it, they realized it would have to wait until our regular Tuesday night meeting, as several people would not be available until then.

It must have been bad timing—a full moon or something—because when the house finally all came together on Tuesday night, we got more than we bargained for.

Everyone gathered in the parlor and began singing a chorus from our scripture song collection, *The Psalter*, but before the refrain ended, Vanessa broke down and sobbingly admitted she was an alcoholic. She offered us a far too detailed explanation of her years of ongoing struggle.

At first, Don and I didn't quite know how to react to this information; we could not understand how a Christian could be an alcoholic. People were sure diving "free-fall" from our perfection pedestal lately.

We were, however, beginning to grasp the validity of the concept of "God placing the solitary (single, lonely) into families," as Psalm 68:6 mentions. The singles needed the influence and presence of families to round out their experience, and we in families needed to make room in our lives to include them. Ultimately, all would benefit.

Vanessa begged for healing and deliverance, so we intervened in the best way we knew how. We seated her in the center of the room, then surrounded her, laying our hands on her and praying lengthily, both in the Spirit and "with understanding." After that extensive ordeal Vanessa's countenance appeared relieved and lightened.

No sooner than we returned to our seats, Jerry had a need to share. Seated cross-legged on the floor just under the pole lamp, he confessed, barely audibly, his addiction to codeine.

From the vantage point of my rocker, I studied his profile as he spoke, realizing I had never really looked at him closely. His black wavy hair curled around his ears and over his collar. The earnest expression on his up-tilted face perfectly caught the glow from the light bulb above; his tears glistened as they flowed down his cheeks. Though he wiped at them, some tears trickled to his chin and then fell, soaking into his red plaid flannel shirt. If my heart had not broken for Vanessa, it certainly did now for Jerry. I wept.

He admitted that at first he merely enjoyed the buzz he got from abusing cough syrups—especially Nyquil, but Vicks or Robitussin would do in a pinch. This had lead to a full-blown requirement for the substance, which caused him to pilfer it from any medicine cabinet, spend all his money on it, and even shoplift as his dependency grew.

He described it as a peaceful, comforting inebriation, but he knew it was wrong and dangerous to be in such bondage. He felt helpless to stop, as he had already tried many times.

We gathered around Jerry, praying for him in much the same manner as we had for Vanessa. One brother received a "word of knowledge" from God, that Jerry was being healed and delivered at that very moment. The brothers agreed to form an alliance of accountability to help Jerry through his recovery, so he wouldn't backslide.

The Holy Spirit's presence in the room was so thick you could cut it with a knife. We felt exhausted and prayed-out as we returned to our seats, expecting to get on with our study time.

Jay, who was seated in the stuffed blue chair opposite me, had been fairly subdued all evening. Now he lifted his bowed head, making eye contact with the group.

Looking heavily burdened, he cleared his throat and began to speak. "I, uh, I don't know quite how to say this," he faltered, "and I don't know if this is the right time. But, I think God wants me to go ahead, because I can't hide my secret any longer." With great effort, he haltingly admitted that he was homosexual.

"I've tried to hide my feelings and tendencies for a long time and I can't anymore," he continued. "I haven't acted on it, but I can't stop the lusting, the desiring and my imaginings." He was sobbing now, begging our forgiveness and desperately in need of our prayers.

Oh, dear God. Not Jay, I thought. He's such a good brother and has such a kind heart. How unfair that he's caught in such a vicious struggle. Tears of compassion streamed down my face for Jay, my rescuer.

"I think I need to move out," he continued, his whole being afflicted under the weight of his sobs. "I'm being unfair to you brothers," his voice and body trembled, "and to myself, if I go on living here, especially in the basement with you guys."

Even though what he said was true, I don't think anyone wanted to admit it. We wanted Jay and we needed Jay; he was an asset both to the leather shop and to the house.

Silently, I wondered which would put him in a less-compromising situation: him living here with temptation but accountability, or him living on his own without it.

We all gathered around him, showing our support and solidarity, and again prayed at length—this time for Jay's victory, healing and direction. As things calmed down and we returned to our chairs, Jon offered Jay the small bedroom off the dining room, saying he himself would move back into the basement. Jay was reluctant to receive such a gracious offer, but we all urged him to stay on and give this a try while he sought God's will. Finally, he lifted his downcast face and agreed to this arrangement.

Many of us gave hugs and words of encouragement to the three confessors, pledging our love and support to see them through their trials.

After being at this for nearly three hours, we were all worn out by the time Jon asked if there were any other needs to be addressed. Everyone pensively looked around the room at one another.

Terry smiled, "Well, I have something that seems pretty insignificant after all this." Then she started to giggle, breaking the somber heaviness of the group. "There's a girl named Vickie who wants to move into the house tomorrow. She has a basset hound. Will that be a problem for anyone?"

Dan had already set the precedent by keeping his mangy dog, Chopper, in the house, thereby breaking the rules and upsetting my feeble attempts at a peaceful existence. Apparently, it was no longer a rule—but merely a suggestion—to not allow pets in the house.

Finding it amusing, we all laughingly agreed that adding a basset hound to the mix was the least of our worries. We voted unanimously to let Vickie and Basil join us.

Pam and Sue graciously offered to share their room with the new girl and her dog. Terry and Ann invited Vanessa to return to their room. And so it was settled.

In closing, we all sang Psalm 133 as Jon and Jay strummed their guitars in unison, "Behold, how good and how pleasant it is for the brethren to dwell together in unity."

And it was.

CHAPTER NINE

MELTDOWN

In the morning, I felt truly encouraged; our renewed harmony of the night before enabled me to continue with the cause of the house. Even though the secrets of many housemates had been exposed, and consequently had to be dealt with, the morale was so improved that I was sure we could make it work.

Just as I finished cleaning up the kitchen, the phone rang. It was my sister, Joyce, calling to say she was coming to visit us in a week-and-a-half. I floated through the next several days, excitedly anticipating her arrival.

Don's life became busier than ever, for all these delicate house issues required his mediation and counsel. He spent many evenings talking with Jerry or Jay. Appropriately, the sisters supported and advised Vanessa, to keep her accountable.

Don continued leading many of our Tuesday night house Bible studies, Wednesday night neighborhood Bible studies, never missed Saturday night coffeehouse and street preaching, and attended regular "leadership meetings" with the church elders. He seemed quite fulfilled by the constant demands of leadership; the busyness didn't bother him a bit.

I realized, all the more, how involvement in ministry must feed a man's ego. He is afforded recognition, a feeling of importance and a sense of accomplishment. It was far easier for him to address others' needs than our personal ones. Our own discussions and decisions were therefore postponed or avoided in the presence of more imminent matters.

While getting ready for bed one night, I told him, "I'm beginning to feel like I'm too low-maintenance. It seems like the only way I can get your attention is if I have problems. We really need to reconnect." But it was not yet to be.

Instead of clamoring for his attention, I began searching the scriptures for advice on how to treat my husband and be more supportive. The teachings at church were along the bias of wives submitting to their husbands and praying for them, behind the scenes, in order for God to honor their own needs. Most of the weekly POP Women's Bible Studies tackled this topic, so it must have been a common concern.

We were taught from the Old Testament that, as a wife, we were to "cleave to our husband," leaving behind the identity we once held in our "father's house." Only then would our King delight in us. (Conversely, I noticed in Genesis 2:24, Adam advised *man* to "leave *his* father and his mother and cleave unto his wife." This seemed a moot point to me since Adam didn't even have parents.)

I'm sure this concept of cutting the apron strings proved helpful in shoring up some of the fragile new marriages, but I believed I had already done this. I didn't keep one foot in my "father's house" as I supposed some of the other young wives did. Living 1,000 miles away from my parents didn't hurt either.

As if he didn't have enough to do, Don wrote a letter to the City of Portland, using his official distinction as head of the Northwest Fellowship. He requested a permit to hold a potluck picnic over Fourth of July weekend at Wallace Park, just a few blocks from Beth Israel. We were granted permission to use a P.A. system, but warned against playing loud music or behaving in any manner that would be disturbing to the peace.

The whole Prince of Peace Fellowship was invited to attend the Sunday afternoon rally, but Beth Israel would host the event. This meant that I had to come up with the menu, most of the food, and organize who was bringing what in order to ensure enough side dishes.

Fortunately for me—and for our kitchen—a new sister named June had just moved in. An outgoing girl with shoulder-length, honey-blond hair, June was the single mother of a baby boy. She had a boyfriend she was trying to break up with because he wasn't a Christian. June liked to cook and made a vat of potato salad for the event, using her own money to buy the ingredients.

June didn't have a job, but money did not seem to be an issue for her. This led me to assume that she received financial support from the boyfriend. And since she didn't have a job, what money she had may have not been considered "income." Perhaps she was merely paying rent to the house.

She brought with her a wooden rocking chair which she spent most of her time in, equally divided between nursing her four-month-old son and avidly crocheting. June also loved vacuuming, a task I gladly delegated to her charge. With a sly wink of her eye, she entrusted me with a valuable hint about vacuuming and men. "Men are easily impressed if, when they come home, they can see the tracks on the carpet of a freshly vacuumed floor. If there's only one bit of housework you do each day, it should be vacuuming. They'll notice it and think you've been slaving hard all day."

Wow, I thought, that's profound. That was one thing my mother had not taught me; though she emphasized vacuuming, I think dusting was more her forte.

The picnic was a huge success. Co-pastor Chuck and his wife, Mary, along with their band (who had recently recorded an album), performed most of their best songs, drawing quite a crowd. People drifted over to join our gathering giving us opportunity to share food and the gospel with them, which was the motive of our outreach. Chuck got into playing some cool trumpet and Mary's engaging voice lilted beautifully through the park.

Don, along with three other men who shared co-pastor Ron's tutelage, each took turns preaching to the crowd. Chuck wrapped it up by inviting those in the crowd to make a personal commitment to

Christ. Many people did, and several of them returned to Beth Israel
with us to spend the night.

One of the new men joining us was named Tom. A burly man in
his mid-30s, Tom was recently divorced and totally "on fire for the
Lord." Another was Johnny, a slight, frail man in his early-70s, which
seemed ancient to us. He was a former jockey, a heavy smoker and
admitted to some health issues, but really had a heart for God and
for the young people at the house.

We were pleased to take them in, as "the Lord was adding daily
those who were being saved," in the same manner as the early church
in the book of Acts. Both men had hearty appetites, so I stretched
our mornings' hot cereals with a little more grain and our evenings'
soups with a little more water.

Additionally, all the church houses were absorbing Gospel
Outreach people, whose ministry conjoined the Prince of Peace while
they were in Portland. These folks—similar to those at our church
in age, look and persuasion—were headquartered at an intriguing
compound called Lighthouse Ranch, in northern California.

They worked their way up and down the west coast in teams,
often taking the "gray rabbit"—a drab, dilapidated bus—which
transported hitchhikers in return for a nominal donation towards
gas. They engaged in migrant farm work and tree planting to support
their missionary endeavors.

We took in one of their team leaders, yet another brother named
Don; he was a mature Christian and a boon to the house.

On Tuesday evening, Johnny wasn't his usual talkative self. He
excused himself prematurely from the table saying, "I'm not feeling
so good. I think I'll go lie down." He reclined in the parlor during
clean-up, continuing to chat with everyone as they passed by.

He insisted on joining us for the house Bible study and sat
up, his fragile frame all but disappearing into the couch cushions.
He requested prayer, and lingered in the parlor with anyone who
was willing to visit with him and explain the ways of God more
thoroughly.

Gradually, everyone else drifted off to their rooms and only Don remained, engrossed with Johnny in a lively biblical discourse.

Around eleven, I came downstairs looking for Don and found him sitting on a chair next to Johnny, who was again reclining on the couch. "I'll just be a few minutes," Don assured me. "I want to sit with Johnny for awhile. He's still not feeling so good." I returned upstairs and went to bed.

About an hour later, Don woke me as he came into our room. "I think Johnny's having a heart attack or something," he whispered. I rose and followed him downstairs where we found Johnny lying on the couch groaning, clutching his chest and left arm with his right hand. Don knelt beside him, laid hands on him and, in authentic POP manner, prayed with a fervency I had never seen in him before.

I went to the kitchen and brought back a glass of water, but Johnny was in too much pain to receive it, or to even acknowledge our presence. His body writhed as he tightly gripped Don's hand. Suddenly his body jerked, twitched a few times, and then he stopped moving altogether.

Don and I froze, our eyes fixed on his lifeless body, fearing Johnny had died. Then we stared at each other for a few moments, afraid to speak of the inevitable. Don placed his ear on Johnny's chest and I felt his wrist for a pulse, which was barely detectible.

"I'm calling Chuck," Don decided, getting to his feet. He walked over to the phone in the foyer. Everyone else in the house was asleep and he didn't want to awaken or alarm them.

"Chuck, this is Don," my husband spoke into the phone following a long pause. I could picture the telephone at Chuck's house ringing incessantly, no doubt waking his whole family. "You remember the old man we brought home with us from Wallace Park? Well, I think he's had a heart attack right here on our couch. What should I do?"

Don listened to his reply, then answered, "Okay, yeah. Uh-huh. Okay. Thanks." He hung up and returned to the parlor.

"What did he say?" I urged. I had been keeping vigil, kneeling at the couch, anxiously watching Johnny while Don was on the phone. "I don't think Johnny's breathing!"

"Chuck says I should do whatever I feel the Lord leads; either continue praying over him, call an ambulance, or both. If he dies I should call the police."

I stared at him and then over at the phone, in disbelief. Wow! I thought. When push comes to shove, we really are on our own here!

"I'm going to stay up and pray for him as long as he needs me," Don resolved. Wearily I trudged back up the stairs. It was nearly daybreak before Don came to bed. I wondered how he was going to make it through his workday with one hour of sleep.

At 6:30, as everyone gathered in the parlor for morning prayer, we found Johnny upright and perky, perched on the couch as though he were now a permanent fixture. His coloring was good and he was talkative as ever, interacting with everyone as they entered the room.

Unable to restrain his excitement until the first song ended, he interrupted and announced to us, "I had the strangest dream last night. I have to tell you all about it. I dreamt that I had a heart attack and died right here on this couch. But God brought me back to life!" He then broke into joyously praising God, and all the housemates joined in.

Don and I looked at each other in dismay. Don turned to him and said, "Johnny, that was no dream. It really happened and I was up with you all night, praying you through."

Johnny's eyes teared up. He rose and practically flung himself onto Don, embracing him. "You're a good brother, a good, good brother. Thank you, thank you," he gushed, weeping. He made his rounds, hugging each and every person in the room, thanking us for being there for him and for taking him in. Then, first one to the dining table, Johnny sat up straight and strong. Brandishing his spoon, he dove into his oatmeal with renewed gusto.

As he calculatedly counted out the grocery money to me on Saturday morning, Jon wore a worried look on his face. "We have 20 adults and three children living here now," he stated flatly. I watched his Adam's apple rise and fall as he swallowed.

"And two dogs, and a partridge in a pear tree," I quipped, wagging my head. But the look on his face told me he was having none of it.

Without cracking a smile, he continued, "I know you're supposed to get $102 for food this week, but we honestly don't have it. All I can afford to give you is $80, so I suggest you go to the co-op. And," he added, in a manner I took as demeaning, "I heard they're giving away government-surplus cheese at Union Gospel Mission on Tuesday morning."

Oh, man—I wanted to say—I pity the poor girl who marries you. But, instead I reminded him, "My sister is coming tomorrow. That'll make 21, and she'll be here for a couple weeks."

"If I can, I'll get you more money later in the week," he bargained.

I walked away, shaking my head and wondering how many housemates were living here absolutely free. If they had no income, the 100% system meant nothing to them. After all, 100% of zero is zero!

I was beginning to get the fretful impression that we were raising a family of 20 on my husband's meager salary. I was forced to live in poverty so that others could be housed and fed. And I certainly didn't relish the idea of standing in a "bread line" at a homeless shelter on Burnside this coming Tuesday morning.

With the meager $80 in my hand, I drove off alone to do the shopping that morning, leaving Don at home with the kids. Benjie seemed a bit sick, so I wanted to get home quickly and not waste time making several stops. Jon wasn't going to tell me what to do, I decided. What did he know about grocery shopping, anyway? I headed straight for Fred Meyer's.

Because of its low price, I resorted to buying "TVP" again, which sold by the pound in Freddie's meat department. While selecting the cheapest grade of ground beef, I was struck with the emotive notion that I could mix hamburger, texturized vegetable protein and oatmeal together in equal parts to make our meatloaves, meatballs and burgers.

June had turned me on to a new food item called ramen noodles. She fixed it for us recently and, not only was it cheap, it was adaptable. She prepared it by adding a bag of frozen mixed vegetables and a couple handfuls of leftover, chopped chicken. At the last minute, she cracked a few eggs into the mix, swirled them around and sprinkled it with soy sauce. Unfortunately, one couldn't serve this tasty "oriental" dish every day or people might get suspicious, but the housemates actually liked it and didn't mind it too often. Bethany even gobbled it up and it was perfect to run through my hand-held, baby-food grinder for Benjie. After searching for awhile, I found them in the soup section. Usually it cost 10 cents a package, which was reasonable, but today I got them for five cents each. What a find!

I hated stooping so low as to use powdered milk; it tasted awful and always had lumps that wouldn't dissolve no matter how hard I stirred. However, June showed me a trick and I tried it. First I beat the milk powder with three cups of water, using an electric mixer, until smooth and frothy. I then transferred that mixture into a gallon pitcher, filling it the rest of the way with water while stirring. Voila! No one could tell the difference. This time I purchased four gallons of milk—instead of eight—deciding that, as we needed it, I would mix it with equal parts prepared powdered milk. This sure helped stretch our milk budget, for we averaged using more than a gallon a day.

I was pleased to again find day-old bread at five loaves for a dollar, so I bought 20. Also, they had day-old peach pies for fifty cents each; I bought three for one night's dessert. Satisfied, I passed through check-out, just grazing my $80 limit. God was truly shopping with me!

Church was filled to overflowing again on Sunday morning. They pushed back the wooden partitions that separated the sanctuary from the coffeehouse and, after filling up that area, people still had to sit on the floor. Many street-people and hippies, some carrying everything they owned in a bedroll on their backs, walked up front and sat cross-legged on the floor around the stage and in the aisles.

Tie-dyed T-shirts, thermal long-underwear shirts, and overalls seemed to be the outfit of choice for the guys. And hats were all the rage; many wore jaunty berets, knit caps or Alpine-style hats with feathers. Most of the women wore mismatched blouses and skirts of paisley, calico or madras plaids. Both men and women wore hiking boots.

Children jostled and babies cried from all corners of the sanctuary. And when the need presented itself, mother's nursed them publicly.

Without realizing the implications of it at the time, we were a cutting-edge church immersed in the throes of a wide-spread revival.

Gospel Outreach proved to be a boisterous crowd. Members of the tree-planting team came up front and led us in their aptly titled *Tree Planter's Song*:

> "Sing unto God, sing praises to His name.
> Sing unto God, sing praises to His name!
> Extol Him that rideth upon the heavens by His name...
> By His name, 'JAH'!
> ...And rejoice before Him..."
> - Psalm 68:4

With hundreds of hands clapping and hundreds of boots stomping on the century-old, wooden floor, our united worship rose to a thunderous crescendo. Our American-Gothic structure was shaken to its very foundation with the reverberations.

The worship flowed beautifully, with singing in the Spirit—including prophecies in tongues—which would then be followed by interpretation. Hands and arms were lifted, reaching and swaying in praise.

There was loud group-prayer, in unknown tongues, with all the voices raised in a suspended din, like the beautiful, babbling frenzy of hundreds of auctioneers. Gradually the exuberance tapered off until a hush fell. At length, a "word of knowledge" or "word of wisdom" would come forth, for the purpose of instructing and encouraging the assembly.

Next, it was time for intercessory prayer, and now that it was July—the peak of America's Bicentennial—we emphasized calling our country to repentance. We "stood in the gap" for our nation's corporate sins, pleading for mercy from a God whom we believed must be about out of patience with our desperately backslidden country.

Praying for personal healing and deliverance was equally vital. The service concluded with a time for those with physical needs to flock up front.

Benjie had been running a fever and woke up covered in a light rash. It was probably just due to prickly heat or roseola but, nevertheless, we took him up front and had him prayed over and anointed with oil. By the time we got home his fever had diminished and he was happy again, though still spotted.

Later that afternoon, our family drove downtown to pick up Joyce at the bus station. She looked cute as she approached us in her gauze peasant-blouse and denim skirt. Suffering from bus-lag after being on the Greyhound for almost twenty-eight hours, every topic we mentioned was hilarious.

We reminisced about the last time she had been to Portland—eleven months earlier—when she came up with our mom, shortly after Benjie was born.

She and Mom had gone to the Apostolic Christian Church the Sunday they were here, while we attended the Prince of Peace. Lucky for us we didn't go with them, for they ended up getting food-poisoning from the thrice-frozen donuts that were served there for "lunch." The lady who served the lunch that day was notorious for thawing and re-freezing her donuts too many times. Poor Joyce and Mom were kept occupied hugging the toilet for the remainder of the day.

Instead of going straight home, we stopped at Baskin Robbins for ice cream cones, stalling for an opportunity to forewarn Joyce about life at Beth Israel.

When we got to the house, Ann and Terry welcomed Joyce into their room, where they had set up a cot and cleared a space for her things. She settled in, toured the house and met the dozen or so housemates who were currently home.

Normally, I wouldn't have cooked for the house on a Sunday, but since Joyce had just arrived, I made a tuna casserole for dinner. Earlier in the week, I had baked and saved aside a loaf of whole wheat bread. Carefully measuring it first, I forced it to yield 14 thin slices and served it with dinner.

I was accustomed to buying our flour at the co-op by now, but last week when I transferred some into the bell jar, I noticed it was crawling with weevils. This grossed me out so badly that I dumped it all. Since everyone commented on how delicious my bread was, I decided to tell my weevils-in-the-flour story. Everyone was amused, so I couldn't resist adding, "Monica would've been okay with the weevils. She would've baked that old flour into bread anyway, saying that God would bless it when we prayed over it!" But I wasn't about to serve weevilly bread to my family and my guest sister. I bought new, whole wheat flour at Freddie's.

All the single brothers made a fuss over Joyce, and she thrived on the attention in her flirtatious, outgoing manner. However, since she was an Apostolic Christian Church member and dating was forbidden, this limited her social life drastically. The guys offered to put her to work at the leather shop so she could "earn her keep," and to occupy her in case she got bored hanging around the house with me every day. I thought it was a poorly disguised plan they hatched in order to spend more time with her. But I didn't mind; I wanted her to enjoy herself.

The next day, Joyce accompanied me and the kids on a pleasant walk through the bustling neighborhood. Not wanting to deny Joyce any part of the unique, northwest Portland experience, I insisted we pay a visit to the Food Co-Op, as well. Besides, I needed more grains, spices and yeast. Of course she had never seen anything like it.

She was fascinated by all the old houses in our inner-city neighborhood—sheltering a stimulating mix of cultists, artists, hippies and the elderly, the latter having lived there for years watching it evolve. We made plans to return soon to browse in some of the artsy boutiques and go out for a snack at Rose's or Quality Pie.

On Tuesday morning, Joyce left the house with the guys, and trotted off to Noah's Ark for the day. I put Benjie in the stroller and, taking Bethany by the hand, we set out for the dreaded food hand-out. It was quite a hike there—over a mile—and was warming up rapidly that morning.

By the time we arrived, the long line was already snaking its way down the sidewalk and around a corner, hugging the aged brick storefronts. After locating its end, we joined the queue. I couldn't help noticing there were not many other young mothers with children. I was surrounded by middle-age to old men and women, all shabbily dressed, some handicapped, and all reeking of stale dirt and body odor.

At first I was disgusted and wondered what on earth I was doing there. But gradually, my heart softened as I stood in solidarity with them for, like it or not, this was my community.

After inching along in that line for over 45 minutes, we finally made it inside the building. There I was given a ten-pound block of cheese (I mentally added grilled cheese sandwiches to the week's menu), a ten-pound box of spaghetti, and one large box each of generic corn flakes and powdered milk. I stuffed my provender into the net carrier under the stroller seat and then went into the adjoining thrift store to use the bathroom.

Benjie was soaked through, but there was no place to change him. Bethany didn't make it in time, so she was going to have a damp walk home. Nearing the front door, I noticed a large bin of toddler-sized clothing for a quarter each. Rummaging through it for a moment, I found a ruffled, sleeveless blouse and pink shorts for Bethany and a striped T-shirt and red shorts for Benjie. As I paid my dollar, I felt thankful that I had accomplished something, both for my family and for the house, that morning.

Though rather unpleasant, the experience, for the most part, was not as horrible as I feared it would be. It was sure hot, though, and the mid-day colors were so clear and vivid that they almost stung my eyes. The noonday sun stood directly overhead as we ambled home, causing us to quickly shed our sweaters. Sunshine filtered through the trees, casting dappled shadows on the sidewalks. We kept crossing the street to stay in the shade.

When she got home from "work" that evening, Joyce told me she had enjoyed her day at Noah's Ark, watching the guys make their wares. They kept her busy manning the phone and the front desk. We held our house Bible study that night and, thankfully, since Joyce was there, had no new issues to address.

Each day the summer heat was building in intensity. The tall, close buildings and the extensive pavement seemed to horde the heat all day, reluctantly releasing it late into the night.

We held our neighborhood Bible study on Wednesday night with the front door open, to catch a fleeting breeze. Several people from the community stopped in to join us.

One of them, a young Asian man who frequented the study, was there. Somewhat of an intellectual, he had a neurological disorder which caused his head to tip to one side, and a facial tic that manifested itself by his constant blinking. His voice carried in an exaggerated monotone, but he was very bright and sincerely inquisitive. He always fired a line of questioning directly at whomever was leading the study, and tonight it was my husband.

Sam kept interrupting as Don attempted to correlate some of the finer points of Paul's epistles—confusing texts regarding the early church's debate over "the circumcision and the uncircumcision." Finally, thoroughly baffled, Sam threw up his hands and interjected, "Don Cremer, uh, would you say, uh, are you saying, uh, that Christians, uh, have funny beliefs?"

Well, this brought down the house! Don just had to shake his head, self-effacingly, and admit, "Yes, Sam. I guess we Christians do have some funny beliefs."

Joyce was flabbergasted by the entire scene. Being a sheltered ACC member, she had never been exposed to such an eclectic assortment of people. This strangely diverse group, made up of both housemates and neighbors, was awash with speaking in tongues and singing in the Spirit. Most were clad in trendy or, at any rate, unconventional hippie garb such as patched overalls, floor-length "granny dresses" and quirky hats.

After the study, many of us went out to sit on the porch and the front stoop, while sipping ice tea and trying to cool off. Joyce wasn't near me when an unfamiliar man sat down beside her. I was trying to keep an eye on her, but I missed noticing him casually place his hand on her knee and slide it up her bare thigh, underneath her modest, denim skirt.

She shrieked—horrified—and slapped at his hand, then stood to her feet, screaming, "I can't take this anymore! You people are all crazy! I'm going home to El Monte, where things are safe and normal!" She ran into the house and stomped upstairs to her room.

I followed, along with a couple other sisters, and we managed to talk her back down, convincing her it was just a temporary freak-out. We assured her that Beth Israel could do that to a person.

Friday evening during dinner, Joyce played her Chuck Girard album on the stereo in the bay window. When the song *Tinajera* came on, Dan began mocking it, using the same annoying voice that he used in his Chopper chant. "Tinajera, Tinajera," he mimicked. "That song is pure sap."

"No, it's not!" Joyce hotly defended it. "This song is very mean-ingful. 'Tinajera' is a term Chuck Girard coined which means 'teenage era.' He's crying out for God to reach the teenage generation."

Not one to stand correction, Dan insisted, "Well, *all* these Christian 'Maranatha' groups are so unprofessional. The only top-quality, Christian band is *2nd Chapter of Acts*. Now, *their* vocals and instrumentals are as good as, or better than, any secular rock group."

When Joyce's record ended, Dan got up and put on the *2nd Chapter of Acts* album, *In the Volume of the Book*, which admittedly was my favorite. "See, now, that's cutting-edge sound… blah, blah, blah…," Dan continued, totally unaware that he had hurt Joyce's feelings.

After dinner, when she and I went out to the kitchen to see if there were any cookies left, we found Gospel Outreach Don lecturing Dan as they loaded the dishwasher.

146

"Responsibility, you see," he was in the middle of saying, "means how you respond, individually, to a situation." He continued reprimanding Dan even after seeing us. "Your attitude matters. Your tongue matters. What you say can cut down or it can build up. That's what I mean by 'accepting responsibility.'"

Surmising that it had to do with Dan and Joyce's tiff, we got out of there fast. Once she realized GO Don had been defending her, Joyce developed a crush on him.

Awhile later, June made a quick run to Freddie's. She returned, all smiles, saying, "I have a surprise for you guys!" She ran back outside and reappeared carrying an inflatable, three-ring kiddy-pool. "This is for second-floor dwellers only," she announced, so we curiously followed her upstairs.

"Where are you going to put that?" Don asked, figuring she might do something crazy like set it up in the landing.

"Out my window, on the front porch roof," she stated, matter-of-factly. The roof was flat; we had crawled out her window onto it several times before, using it as a patio. It just might work.

Don, Joyce, our kids and I all followed June into her room, which faced the street. Handing me her baby, she opened the tall, double-hung window and climbed out. Don and Joyce proceeded in her wake, and soon the three were engaged in blowing up the three tiers of the pool. The kids and I watched them from inside.

Presently, June reappeared through the window. "I have one more thing to bring in. Can you hold Joshua another minute?" she asked.

I laughed out loud at the thought of a swimming pool on the roof. This was too much! June was a genius! She knew how to cut right through all the stress and crap by adding fun and recreation. Maybe my problem was I had been taking this house way too seriously.

In an instant she returned with a webbed, patio lounge-chair she had just bought for herself. "But how are you going to fill the pool?" I puzzled.

"I bought a new hose. There's a spigot right beside the front porch stairs." She was right, there was. A skimpy piece of worn, leaky hose was currently attached to it. Don had used it to wash

147

our car on the rare occasion that we snagged a parking space close enough to reach it.

In a flash she was outside again, this time extending the hose up to Don as he lay near the roof's edge with his arm reaching downward. With a flick of the faucet, we had water and Don began filling the pool.

It wasn't long before we were all in it. June was already wearing a tank top and cut-offs, Joyce was in her respectable, divided-skirt culottes and Don and I just rolled up our pant-legs. We put the kids in too, gingerly wetting their feet at first. Soon everyone was splashing and giggling with delight.

When Terry and Ann returned home from a movie around 9:30, they were shocked to find us all on the porch roof outside their window. "Allo, what's this?" Terry piped up playfully, poking her head out at us. They both shrugged and decided to climb out their window and join us.

"How many people do you think this roof can hold?" Ann questioned, cautiously.

"Well, I guess we'll find out," laughed June.

All too soon, darkness cloaked the neighborhood. Don and I reluctantly left the rooftop party and brought our kids inside to put them to bed. The sisters stayed out there cooling off in the balmy, mid-summer evening breeze until late into the night. We drifted off to sleep lulled by the drone of their distant chatter and occasional bursts of laughter.

Judy holds Bethany and Benjamin at Silver Falls,
as housemates slide down the waterfall in the background.

CHAPTER TEN

NIGHT FALL

In the morning, Joyce announced, "Last night we decided we want to go to Silver Falls today. June and Ann can go, but Terry can't." Terry usually worked a short shift at Meier and Frank's on Saturdays.

"Sure!" Don and I agreed. "It looks like a perfect day for it." The sky was clear as a bell and it was warming up beautifully. We decided to invite others in the house to join us, and I got busy making sandwiches to take with us. June dashed to Freddie's for the luxuries: canned soda pop and potato chips.

Twelve people ended up going, so we took two cars. Ann, Tom and Portland State-student Don rode in Kirk's jeep, while we squeezed our kids up front with us and put Joyce, Gospel Outreach Don, June and her baby in our backseat.

A little more than an hour into the drive, we passed through the town of Silverton. On the outskirts, en-route to the park and falls, I pointed out to Joyce a former Apostolic Christian Church from our childhood. The quaint, white farmhouse—which had once evoked such fervent emotions of hatred and dread in us—was no longer used as a church.

Throughout my childhood, until my parents moved us to California in 1966, my dad had serviced this church with pulpit supply every third Sunday. There was only a handful of elderly church members, and occasionally some of their family members, attending there. Rarely were there any kids for us to hang out with and we dreaded the long, boring drive.

Thus we inequitably despised the mandate to go there every three weeks, taking turns with the other two ministers who were both my uncles. We cousins exaggerated our horror stories of "going to Silverton," trying to outdo each other with our renditions of car-sickness, family spats and ingenious threats of jumping from a moving car. Anything to avoid Silverton!

Joyce and I laughed as we recounted these memories and marveled at how innocent the small, frame structure now looked, after time had wedged a few years and degrees of separation between us. We realized we had never appreciated the beautiful scenery in the area, for even when we attended Apostolic Christian Church picnics held at Silver Falls, we were too consumed by our hatred of going to Silverton to even notice.

Once at the park, we hiked the three-mile trail back to the falls, taking turns carrying the little ones. The vistas were breathtaking and before long we decided unanimously that we were "nature freaks."

The brothers went swimming, wearing cut-offs, but none of the sisters wanted to swim. Even during the hottest summer days, Oregon's creeks and rivers, clinging to their Cascade origins, remain freezing cold. Besides, I wasn't about to let the housemates see me in a swimsuit. Joyce hiked in her token, ACC-permitted culottes, a compromise reached by members still obeying their "no-pants" rule, but inconvenienced by a solid diet of skirts.

At one point on the trail, while GO Don was carrying Benjie on his shoulders, Joyce asked me if she could borrow my camera. She ran to catch up with GO Don and stopped him, saying,—as if to the baby—"Oh, you look so cute! Here, let me take your picture!" He paused for a moment, bouncing the baby to get him to laugh. After he was out of ear-shot, Joyce slyly confided to me, "And I *didn't* mean Benjie!" Yes, I couldn't help but agree with her. GO Don was an appealing guy.

Sunday afternoon, several of us walked up into the hills west of our neighborhood, in search of the Pittock Mansion. The castle-like, stone structure was once home to a Portland business magnate. Jon, Ted, Jay and others, who had not been able to go with us on Saturday, joined us for this outing.

Joyce wore her denim skirt with navy blue tights underneath, which turned out to be a big mistake. The more we walked, the more they sagged, requiring her to stop every few steps and pull up the drooping hose. The steeper we climbed, the more constant the tugging, until finally the crotch drooped down below her knees causing her to walk like a penguin.

Suddenly she stopped right in the middle of the road and, with all of us watching, removed her shoes and slipped out of the sweaty tights. She tied the stretched out "legs" around her waist, letting the "panty" part hang down behind her. To the amazement of all, she continued the hike like that!

The guys teased her, saying that it was obvious she felt comfortable enough around the housemates now to "let her tights down."

Joyce's stay proved rejuvenating for me. It was like a breath of fresh air having a family member visit from afar. It made me feel that Beth Israel was actually my home; I could entertain family and not be totally embarrassed.

I think it also provided a welcomed reprieve for the house members. They tried to be on their best behavior, rather than at each others' throats, when she was around. She continued going to work each morning at Noah's Ark and sometimes they even let her help work on their leather projects.

That Thursday Don took off work, as he had a dental appointment in the morning and several errands to run in the afternoon. Returning to the house around noon, he was approached by a young man who may have been one of the half-way house residents.

"Hey, man!" the guy called out, catching Don in mid-flight as he bounded up the steps. "Can you help me? I, uh, I need some money." He kept his eyes downcast, focusing on his shuffling feet.

"I don't have any money," Don replied, "but if you want to come inside, I'll give you some lunch." The man, a little older than Don, followed him up the stairs and into the house. I was in the kitchen making peanut butter and jelly sandwiches for the kids when Don poked his head in the doorway. "I'm back," he announced.

"Hi!" I turned my head to greet him. "Do you want me to make you a sandwich?"

"Sure," Don answered, "and one for my friend here, too, okay?"

It was then that I glanced down the hallway and noticed a man with greasy, matted black hair cowering in the foyer.

Don took him into the dining room via the parlor, rather than bringing him through the kitchen. I carried two glasses of ice water out to them as they were being seated at the table. The man didn't look up at me but kept his gaze fixed steadily on his lap. Though he wasn't moving, his body twitched.

"Do you know the Lord?" Don plunged right in. Don must have nabbed his Bible from the parlor table as they walked through the room, for he now had it spread open on the table between himself and the man. The man made an indistinguishable grunting sound.

Returning to the kitchen, I quickly put together two bologna sandwiches, placing them on plates, accompanied by several carrot sticks. I brought the plates into the dining room and set them in front of the two men. Don thanked me, but the man was silent.

I sat down with my kids at the nook table and stirred carob powder into the milk in their sippy-cups. It sounded like Don was leading the man down the "Roman Road" in explaining the gospel but each time he mentioned the words Jesus or Christ, the man let out a deep groan.

Realizing they needed their privacy, as did the kids and I, I got up and kicked the doorstop, allowing the swinging door to close and separate us. The man hadn't touched his lunch and was on his feet now, scuffling and uttering guttural sounds as Don recited scripture.

"The gift of God is eternal life," Don was saying, pointing at the passage, "through Jesus Christ our Lord."

"Aaahhhh!" the man moaned, flailing his arms and revealing deep perspiration rings in the armholes of his wrinkled, blue, button-down shirt.

Don grabbed at the man's arms. "Here, sit down and eat," he motioned, pulling his chair out further for him. The man emitted a strange, pungent odor—a repulsive mixture of sweat, body odor and something chemical-ish that I couldn't identify. It was permeating the house.

I chattered to my children to drown out the noise coming from the dining room. Glad to find Benjie's Fisher-Price toy characters on the floor under his highchair, I began playing with them on the table to distract the kids. My kids didn't seem at all concerned that there was a screaming lunatic less than ten feet away. The closed door and the presence of their parents was all that shielded them, but apparently that was enough.

I heard Don continuing, undaunted, "We are all sinners and Christ died to reconcile us to God." The man's volume escalated in response. The kids and I proceeded eating our sandwiches and seedless grapes.

"If you confess the name of the Lord Jesus...," Don was saying, and then his voice was overcome by a louder outcry. I heard more scuffling followed by what sounded like a chair falling over. I got up and peeked into the dining room. Maybe he needed my help. Don's left hand tightly grasped at the man's writhing hands in order to hold them together, while he attempted to place his right hand on the man's head; all the while he was praying in a bold, authoritative tone.

"In the name of Jesus," Don commanded, "you spirits of oppression and torment, come out of this man's body!"

"AAAHHHHH!!" the man roared, flailing at Don, then he turned and beat his fists against the wall.

"Oh, Father God!" Don countered, "In the name of Jesus, and by the power of your Holy Spirit, I pray for your peace and healing to flood this man right now. Demons, you have no power here! You will torment him no more!"

The man let out the loudest, ugliest scream I had ever heard, then slumped, falling face down on the floor. Still kicking and flailing like a toddler throwing a tantrum, his voice gradually lowered and his body calmed as Don knelt beside him, praying softly.

Presently, the man looked up at him and attempted to rise, allowing Don to help him. When he began quietly weeping, Don handed him his bandana handkerchief and again invited him to resume eating his lunch. As the man cautiously began eating, I could hear Don's voice gently reading scripture to him. There were no more outbursts.

I kept the children occupied with toys and chatter as they finished their lunch. I was amazed at how they seemed to not even notice the disturbance. God had so graciously protected them from any fear or harm that I couldn't help but marvel.

Several minutes later, Don poked his head in from the hallway and said that all was well. He had escorted the man out and walked him down the street. "The guy didn't say much," Don reported, "but he seemed like a whole different person after that encounter." Don went on his way rejoicing as he ran his errands that afternoon. I rehearsed my part: keeping the door locked and hoping the man wouldn't return.

Whew, I thought, at least Joyce missed that one! We decided it would be wise not to mention the exorcism to her when she returned from working at Noah's Ark, lest she be alarmed—or worse yet, take the story home with her.

That evening we took her out to dinner at Rose's Delicatessen. A cousin of ours, who had an apartment in the northwest district, worked there now. It was fun seeing her at Rose's and, being an accomplished baker herself, she told us how much she enjoyed working there surrounded by their famous seven-layer chocolate cakes and six-inch tall cheesecakes.

Friday morning I took Don to work because I needed the car. Around noon, after Joyce had finished packing, I drove her over to our aunt and uncle's house. Joyce planned to spend the final week of her vacation with her favorite cousin, a girl her age who was also an Apostolic Christian Church member.

With our departure from the ACC still so current in her mind, my aunt—a devout member—chose to follow the edict of "shunning." This was the prescribed method of treatment toward those who had once been members of their church but had chosen to leave.

When I entered their house, along with Joyce and my children, she barely acknowledged my presence. She had not seen Benjamin since he was a newborn and my mom had visited last August. She always adored Bethany, so she now lavished attention on both of the kids.

Joyce would be gone all week, going with them to their church and activities, and I knew I would miss her. I anticipated seeing her again on Friday, for I planned to pick her up and take her back to the bus station.

The Noah's Ark leather crew had made Joyce a custom Bible cover, engraved with their pet name for her—the word "Rejoice!" They had presented her with this thoughtful appreciation gift the day before, which was her last day working there. She excitedly showed it to our aunt and cousin, then slipped her favorite Bible into it. She used it for many years to come.

Around noon on Saturday, just after we had returned from grocery shopping, Tom rushed into the kitchen announcing, "We've got a live one, Don!" Don dropped everything, leaving me to put away the groceries and prepare lunch for the kids. He ran out to the foyer to join Tom in ministering to a pair of Jehovah's Witnesses who were at the door.

Inviting them into the parlor, Don engaged them in a lengthy, lively tirade. Though there were two, one of the Jehovah's Witnesses did most of the talking. This man insisted that the only way one could find favor with God was to read and study the Bible, because knowledge was the key to salvation. According to his interpretation of the book of Revelation, he believed only 144,000 people would be "saved."

Don told them about the grace of God and the gift of God—our salvation through Jesus—but the indoctrinated devotee discounted this information, clinging to his pet doctrines. Tom watched in rapt attention, sometimes putting in his two-cents-worth, but allowing Don to lead, as Don was his current mentor.

Finally, Don asked them if they were confident they would go to heaven when they died. They answered that no, they were not. Without missing a beat, Don inserted the clincher, "And you want to take me with you?"

The hot weather continued and those "dog days" brought out the weirdos in droves. That same night Pam offered to stay home and baby-sit Benjie, so Bethany and I accompanied Don to Noah's Ark. Of course Don wasn't there long, as he took a team and headed downtown to preach.

On these long, hot summer nights everyone seemed to be outside. The line at a popular downtown theater, continuously showing *Rocky*, provided a captive audience as it trailed down the block and around the corner. Since no one dared vacate their place in line, Don, Ron and other street preachers proclaimed the gospel and handed out tracts to the ensnared crowd.

Using their tattered telephone book as a booster chair, I situated little Bethany at one of Noah's Ark's recycled, phone-cable-spool tables. I sat down beside her, appreciating the chance to cool off in the air-conditioned coffeehouse.

A third chair at our table was empty, and throughout the evening, several diverse characters took turns joining us. While Bethany and I were sharing a bowl of popcorn and drinking a cinnamon-orange concoction we called Russian Tea, a transvestite seated himself at our table. He politely engaged my toddler and me in a conversation.

"Do you come here often?" he asked me in a husky New York accent.

"Yes," I managed, "in fact, I live at the house that runs this place."

"Oh, that's nice," he said, and then turning to Bethany he added, "What a sweet little girl. What's your name, little girl?" Bethany glanced at him shyly, but kept on eating her popcorn, so I answered for her.

She was intently watching the band, as Dan was singing, and she recognized him. Bethany was fond of Dan, but she especially loved the drums. What she really wanted to do was wander up on the stage, but I restrained her.

She expressed no fear of the person at our table though he was flamboyantly decked in a curly, black wig, heavy make-up, bright dress and red-feather boa. I marveled at the innocence and acceptance exhibited by children. No wonder Jesus wanted us to have unconditional, unbiased love like that of a little child. I thanked God again for proving Himself faithful to surround our children with a hedge of protection.

Maybe the man's husky voice didn't alarm Bethany for another reason: strangely enough, he sounded similar to her other grandma—Don's mom—whom she had just seen in May.

Before he rose to leave, I summoned up the courage to hand him a tract and found myself feebly mouthing, "God loves you."

He accepted it and, tucking it into the top of his padded bra, he rasped, "Thanks, Hon, that's always good to know." Rising to his stiletto-heeled feet and swishing the red boa about his shoulders, he adjusted his tawdry dress and teetered out the door, into the night.

Next to occupy the chair was a member of the Holy Order of MANS, arrayed in his authentic white, biblical-style, wraparound robe. They were a Gnostic cult—allegedly founded by the apostle Thomas—basing their religion on knowledge and reason alone, even to the omission of faith.

Bethany beckoned me to put my ear toward her mouth and she whispered, "Mommy is that Jesus?" This man didn't speak to us and he didn't stay long.

Four Hare Krishna members were seated at a nearby table, wearing their bright orange sarongs and bells. They spoke in hushed tones amongst themselves and seemed to be enjoying the music. Many of their group frequented the coffeehouse and were always welcome to stay, so long as they didn't proselytize.

By and by, Don returned and joined our table. He'd had quite a wild night himself. "I was standing in front of a bar, preaching," he related, "as a whole gang of bikers rode up and parked in front of me. This one guy started tenderly polishing his bike, so I told him that if he loved God as much as he loved that bike, he'd be saved when everything else was gonna burn." Don laughed and then continued, "The guy totally misunderstood me and came right up into my face. Shaking his fist, he said, 'I'm gonna go into that bar and I'm gonna do me some drinkin' and if I come out here and find my bike burnin', I'm gonna kill you!'"

Next, Don recounted how a man in the theater line appeared to express some interest as he and Nick pummeled the crowd. "The man motioned to Nick and said, 'Hey, come here. I want to ask you something.' Nick was excited, hoping the man would pose a deep question that would spark a theological debate. 'I wanna know...' began the man, in all seriousness. 'I wanna know... where'd your friend get his pants?'" Immediately all eyes in the crowd shifted their attention to Don's gray-and-blue-striped, flair-leg slacks!

"But there was some 'fruit,'" Don shook his head and continued. "Last week I was preaching near the downtown building that has that huge neon 'Jesus Saves' sign on top of it. God seemed to impress on me to face a certain window in that office building as I preached, so I did. Then I prayed for the people who worked in that building."

"Well, tonight," he concluded, "I was on that same street corner when some guy in the theater line said to me, 'You know, I work in that building right there (he indicated by pointing to the very same one) and I've always ignored that sign on top. But one day last week, I thought about it when I saw someone preaching down here—I think it was you. God really touched my heart, so I decided right then and there to ask Jesus to be my Lord and Savior.'" Don was jazzed!

On the heels of such an eventful coffeehouse night, naturally, we took several people home with us to Beth Israel.

The next morning, church was packed to the rafters again. Chuck announced that we would have a time of sharing and testimonies rather than a regular service. In turn, many congregants stood and recounted their recent or dramatic salvation experiences as the microphone was passed around.

Everyone cheered as a young woman, visiting from another church, relayed her astounding tale of being completely healed of cancer.

Next, a kid named Derek, whom I recognized as having spent the night at Beth Israel, was not to be outdone. He rose and, with a winning grin, began describing the remarkable story of his skiing accident six months earlier—an accident which had left him with several broken bones, and paralyzed from the waist down. He stroked his buzz-cut, blond hair nervously, as he concluded by saying that upon becoming a Christian, he had been instantly healed of all these injuries. Everyone clapped and praised God for this testimony. He was outgoing and soaked up the attention like a sponge.

I spoke with my cousin after church let out, and she elaborated on her plans to "put up" tomatoes from her ripening, communal house garden. Furthermore, the brothers at her house were going to pick cherries for her to can. The whole topic was beginning to irk me as I considered Beth Israel's neglected plot of land, now a jungle of five-foot weeds.

During the conversation, I realized that I had never even had occasion to visit *our* backyard. I merely eyed it with distaste each time I went on the back porch to fetch the broom, mop, or step-stool. None of *our* brothers were inclined to clean up our yard, let alone harvest produce.

Also vexing me was the fact that we kept receiving delinquent notices on our car insurance and medical bills. Don had been reticent to confront Jon about the issue, but at my insistence he finally did so that afternoon. Here we were being divested of *all* our money, yet our needs were not being met as prescribed.

Sunday was free-day for dinner, but so many people were hanging around the house that afternoon, I sensed they were expecting to be fed. I stood before the open freezer, reveling in the blast of cool air and considering the possibilities.

I suspiciously eyed, for the umpteenth time, the generous bag of smelt that had been donated to the house. I was unfamiliar with cooking fish, so I had merely allowed it to consume valuable freezer space for a couple months.

I asked June if she had any ideas on how to prepare the bony, useless fish. These four-to-five-inch critters seemed like more work than they were worth. She suggested we barbeque them and have a big "smelt feed" for the house and neighborhood.

Truly inspired, she zipped over to Freddie's to buy an outdoor grill, charcoal and lighter fluid. I dumped the pile of fish onto the kitchen counter, breaking apart the frozen mass so they would thaw faster. I recruited several brothers to decapitate and de-fin the slippery, stinky fare. Meanwhile, I got busy peeling, chopping and frying a ten pound bag of potatoes, meting them out into two big skillets.

It was murderously hot and muggy that afternoon. Ted opened the back door to get some airflow and announced that the thermometer, nailed onto the shaded porch wall, stood at ninety-six degrees. I estimated the humidity to be about that high, too, especially in our crowded, fishy kitchen. But the brothers jostled each other, laughing and talking and animating the fish, the smoke rose from my pans of browning potatoes, and life was good once more.

June surprised us by bringing a brown-paper grocery bag full of corn-on-the-cob into the kitchen. I gasped and smiled at her. "Wow! I sure appreciate the way you've made this house seem more like a home! First a wading pool on the roof and now a cook-out on the front porch!" Don tore into shucking the corn, bringing it to a boil in our largest roaster.

The smelt cooked up quickly on the outdoor grill; about a dozen reposed on the grate at one time. Several neighbors joined us on the stoop and porch, lured by the barbecue aroma wafting down Hoyt Street. We put Chuck and Mary's *Little Child* album on the record player, pulled the two speakers as far into the parlor as possible, and blasted the music loud enough to hear it out on the front porch.

At dusk, Sue brought down two large packages of sandwich cookies from her room and passed them around. She put on a pot of her infamous "cowboy coffee." Without having a coffee maker, it was the best we could do.

Her technique was to pour a liberal mound of ground coffee into a large saucepan, fill it with water and, after bringing it to a brisk boil, turn it down on low. As it simmered, the grounds would sink to the bottom leaving a strong—almost syrupy—brew, which we would then pour through a tea strainer into our cups. As if the crowd wasn't lively enough, we were now energized by a java jolt!

Getting to sleep that night was next to impossible; everyone was too hot and uncomfortable, not to mention wired. The attic was an absolute oven, so Kirk made a late-night run to his parents' house to borrow a box-fan. Situating it at the top of the attic stairway brought some relief to the dorm-dwelling brothers.

Don and I didn't own a fan and had no money to buy one, so the best thing we could do was to prop up our rear-facing, screenless window with our hefty *Strong's Concordance of the Bible*. We kept the door to the kids' room open for ventilation.

A few hours later, the slightest hint of a breeze arose, breaking up the heavy stillness of the night. Suddenly there was an enormous "BANG!!!" like an explosion or a shotgun blast, directly over our heads. Don and I sprang out of bed, instantly on our feet.

That sound was immediately followed by the loud clatter of glass shattering right above us. Immediately, we read each others' minds and feared the worst: someone in our attic had either shot himself or shot someone else!

Instantaneously, we heard a shuffling overhead, then a loud thud followed by a moaning cry, then more scuffling. And then, "Boom!!" something hit the attic floor.

By now Don was climbing into his jeans and I had thrown on my robe. The commotion continued, as though someone was limping, falling and then being dragged across the rough floor.

We flew out of our room like a shot and, along with all the other frightened, second-floor dwellers, crowded into the landing. Apparently the door from the landing to the attic stairs had been left ajar for air circulation. From the top of the stairs there came another crash, an anguished male voice moaning, and then another thud on the floor, followed by a cry of pain.

We all stood there frozen to our spots, watching in horror as a blanket-shrouded mass bounced and rolled its way down the steps. It hit the attic door with such force that it sprang wide open, slamming into the door of the adjacent bathroom. A writhing, human-size bundle deposited itself onto the floor of the landing, directly at our feet.

I screamed and cowered backwards, shutting the door to our kids' room and standing guard in front of it, hoping to protect them from the deranged killer. Don, apparently still half asleep, surveyed the scene and then fled down the stairs, taking them two at a time. He flung open the front door and stood beside it as a sentry, waiting, guarding.

The bundle on the landing floor stumbled in its attempt to raise itself to its feet. We all caught our breath as a body emerged from the blanket it was wrapped in. His covering slipped from his grip and fell to the floor, exposing his nakedness. He grabbed at the blood-stained blanket, lifted it from the floor and attempted to tie it around his waist.

I bounded to the bathroom, wetting several wash cloths as I barked out instructions for him to lie down on the floor. His head was bleeding profusely and his face, hands and chest were streaming with blood. I packed the cold cloths all over his head as several brothers ran downstairs to retrieve plastic bags of ice from the kitchen.

The victim was Derek, the young kid we had brought home from the coffeehouse on Saturday night—the one with the miraculous healing testimony at church. He couldn't have been more than 18.

Presently, as no perpetrator burst down the stairs to flee the house, Don closed the front door and crept sheepishly back upstairs. I glanced at him out of the corner of my eye, noting his return.

I continued running back and forth from the bathroom, wringing out blood and re-wetting the cloths for Derek's head. I knelt beside him, trying to keep his trembling body covered, hoping he wouldn't go into shock. One of the sisters put towels under his head to protect the carpet, while another sister wiped the blood from his hands, arms and chest. Some of the brothers went up in the attic to survey the scene and start cleaning up the broken glass.

"Where were you?" I glared at Don. "Why did you run downstairs and leave me and the kids up here? I can't believe you did that!"

"I thought somebody shot someone and they'd be running downstairs and out of the house," Don snapped back.

"Oh, that's just great!" I fumed. "So you left me and the kids up here, defenseless against what you thought was an armed gunman?"

I don't think anyone in the house had ever heard us bickering before, but I didn't care. The trauma of the situation, coupled with the hour of the night, had left me vulnerable enough to publicly scold my husband. I knew this was something the "godly wife" should never do, but I was mad. "I just can't believe it!!" I repeated, in disgust.

When Derek's bleeding stopped, his body had been stabilized and his wounds bandaged, we helped him sit down on the bottom step of the attic stairway. Still clad only in his blanket, he unfolded to us his tale:

Upon preparing to bed down, he had moved three of our couch cushions beneath the attic window at the rear of the house, to lie down on. He then opened the double-hung window at his head, as widely as possible, in order to get some air-flow.

For some reason, just as the breeze kicked up, the weights in the window sash broke. This caused the window to slam shut, instigating the initial "bang." The window pane shattered into a million pieces all over his face and chest.

The shock of the noise and the falling glass caused him to jump up, but when he did, he hit his head squarely on a rafter above him, splitting his head open. Disoriented by pain and darkness, he cried out and fell forward onto the floor, gashing his forehead and bloodying his nose.

Realizing he was bleeding and needed help, and aware of his nakedness, he grabbed his blanket to cover himself and groped his way toward the stairs. The blanket became entangled around his feet, causing him to fall again, so he threw it over his head, cocooning himself in it to keep it off the floor.

He knocked the fan over, then misjudging the first step, he tripped and fell onto the stairway and rolled down the entire flight. Becoming more ensnared in the blanket as he rolled, he crashed into the door. It flew open, depositing him—a bloody mess, on the floor of the landing—at the feet of his startled witnesses.

Finally, with the disaster averted and most of the mess cleaned up, we all made our way back to our respective rooms in an attempt to salvage what was left of the night. In the morning, though bandaged and bruised, Derek obediently accompanied the brothers to the leather shop.

On Tuesday night, at our house meeting, Derek made a disturbing confession. He admitted that the entire story he had told at church—the skiing accident, broken bones, paralysis, and subsequent miraculous healing—had been fabricated to get attention. He had made the whole thing up.

Apparently his accident in the attic was sobering enough to instill the fear of God in him. He stated that he felt compelled to confess his spurious tale. He volunteered to leave Beth Israel the following morning and no one tried to stop him.

CHAPTER ELEVEN

BUGGED

Later that same Wednesday morning, I packed up Bethany and Benjamin for a walk to the co-op. I was tired and cranky from our recent crises and it was another relentlessly hot day. Even inside the gloomy old building there was no relief.

I needed peanut butter, so I began digging into the vat with a scoop and placing it into my bell jar. Today, maybe due to the heat, their peanut butter was way too runny. This aggravated me because it was never a smooth, spreadable consistency. It was either so thick that I had to jab at it and it tore the bread when spreading, or it was too thin and would ooze out of a sandwich.

Bethany refused to stay near me and the stroller; she kept running off to hide in other aisles. I was afraid she would inch her way out the door and disappear into the surging noon-hour rush. I repeatedly had to leave the stroller and my items to go hunt her down and bring her back. Benjie, at almost a year old, was no better. He concocted Houdini-like tricks in his effort to slip out of his stroller restraints.

"Oh, forget it!" I finally muttered to the peanut butter, forcefully replacing the lid and setting the jar down on the cement floor.

Next, I moved my procession over to the huge barrel of honey, put my honey jar in place on the floor, and opened the spigot. As the honey flowed, quickly filling my bell jar, I observed that it, too, was runny. A little more forgiving, I excused it as also due to the heat. As the level approached the top, I squatted beside my jar, grabbed the back of my wandering daughter's shirt with one hand and closed the spigot with the other.

But something didn't look right; even in the dimly lit store I could tell there were crumbs of some kind in the honey. I started to screw the lid on anyway, and then leaned in to get a closer look. The crumbs were moving! The honey was swimming with big, fat, black ants!

"That does it!!" I ranted to nobody in particular. "I've had it with this place. This stuff is crap!" Leaving the peanut butter jar where it stood and abandoning the open, infested honey jar, I clasped my daughter's hand under mine, onto the stroller handle, and marched out of the co-op.

We retraced our steps back past our house, and then hoofed it all the way over to Fred Meyer's. There I bought regular peanut butter and regular honey, the way regular people do.

I was never going back to that stupid co-op again. They can have their ants and their weevils and their bare feet on their bare floor, I thought. But, I, for one, am part-and-parcel to it no more!

Friday evening as we were finishing dinner, my uncle brought Joyce and her stuff back over to Beth Israel. We wanted to see her once more and take her to the bus station ourselves. Since there was no place to park out front, he double-parked his car while unloading her bags. Don and I both went out to put her things into our trunk.

I asked my uncle if he would like to come in and see the house but, due to the lack of a parking spot as well as his own reluctance, he declined. Always kind and encouraging, though, he did say that it looked like a nice place and he hoped we were happy there.

I was actually glad he hadn't come into the house, because by then we had a new problem: fleas. Earlier in the day, June announced that she had found flea bites on her ankles and on her baby. It was inevitable due to those pesky dogs. I knew they should have never been allowed in the house. Now we all had to suffer.

Fortunately, Vickie and her basset were moving out this weekend. The lucky girl had been accepted into the prestigious, all-female Shiloh House, a Christian ministry housed in a stately mansion in the lovely Laurelhurst district. Known for its lush amenities and good reputation, there usually was a waiting list.

Soon, too, it would be "good riddance" to Chopper—the bane of my existence—as Dan was preparing to go to Central America with a Gospel Outreach team. Guatemala had recently suffered a devastating earthquake, so GO seized the opportunity to do relief work and share the gospel with the needy there.

June had already gone to the store for flea powder. She planned to sprinkle it lavishly over all the carpeted areas, leave it on overnight, and then thoroughly vacuum the whole shebang in the morning.

I told Joyce about the fleas as she traipsed up our stairs for the last time. We both laughed with relief, glad she would get to miss out on that little adventure. I wasn't about to relate all the horror stories of the disruptions she had missed during the past week. I was actually glad that she had been at our cousin's instead of here during all that nonsense. Whew! Maybe our credibility had been saved.

After she said her brief goodbyes to those housemates who were home, our family drove her downtown to the bus station and saw her off at 7:30. She said she'd had so much fun during her visit that she intended to return to our beloved Portland again next year. Both she and I shed tears as we parted.

When we got back to the house, Tom passed us in the foyer, laden with a bundle of his bedding. He matter-of-factly announced to us that he had lice and he needed my help. He wanted to launder all of his clothing and linens in the hottest water available.

Well, Joyce's departure had certainly been timely! I wished *I* could escape some of the absurdity of this house, but every time I turned around, there was a new challenge to face, a new crisis to handle. If I dared to entertain any inkling of being persnickety, this buggy day would have put an end to that!

Don herded the kids upstairs—allowing Benjie to crawl up the stairs by himself on all fours—and got them ready for bed. I led Tom to the basement and started the washing machine for him. I didn't want to touch any of Tom's laundry and sincerely hoped the lice had not spread to anyone else in the house. At least he doesn't room on our floor, I thought. Regardless, I began imagining that I itched all over.

Later that evening, when we located Jon, and Don handed his paycheck over to him, I seized the opportunity to voice my decision about the Food Co-Op.

"I'm never going back into that place again! There were ants in the honey today. I'm sick of finding weevils in the flours and grains, too. If *you* want to continue shopping there, then keep your membership. Otherwise, you may as well cancel it, 'cuz it's not gonna be me." I pursed my lips, suppressing the urge to belt out Bob Dylan's lyrics, "It ain't me, babe. It ain't me you're lookin' for."

Jon stared at me in disbelief and started to object, "But you *have* to shop there. Everything's natural and organic and, besides, we can't afford to *not* make use of it."

I just kept shaking my head. I wasn't going to budge on this one. Silently fuming, he tallied my grocery allotment, again giving me less than I expected.

"Vickie is leaving tomorrow," he offered in explanation, "and Pam's out of here in a few days. Dan's moving into a different house before he goes to Guatemala. So, that's three less people. Besides, Gwen plans to come here and make dinner on Monday night."

He handed me a measly $72 dollars. Okay, I thought, I can handle this. Almost daily we were being given a plethora of fresh zucchini and other vegetables from the gardens of people at church. I would continue incorporating them into every dinner to augment our meals. And once again, God was going to have to do a miracle with my shopping.

Sunday at church, I passed out the invitations I had made for Benjamin's first birthday party. I would hold the party that next Friday, as a luncheon, inviting all the little ones his age from church.

Last spring and summer there had been quite a population explosion at the Prince of Peace, with the birth of 13 boys and two girls. The church nursery was packed with all those babies. We nursing mothers had to sit in the chairs in shifts and the babies napped two or three to a crib. We often discussed possible reasons why there may have been so many boys born in 1975. Could it mean a war was going to break out in 17 or 18 years?

Recently, Benjie had decided on his own that his breastfeeding days were over. He had been gradually losing interest, so I had weaned him down to just nursing in the morning and at night. He was taking to his sippy-cup pretty well. I was satisfied to have nursed my second baby for a year. Nursing Bethany had not been as successful due to her premature birth, jaundice and colic. Benjie was beginning to walk now, a step or two at a time, before dropping to the floor and resorting to his speedier crawl.

On the morning of his birthday, I dressed him in his light blue overalls and a white T-shirt. He had crawled into June's room to play with her son, who was just mastering sitting up. June held Benjie's hands and aimed him back towards me, then I knelt and coaxed him to come. The birthday boy walked across the landing alone for the first time, straight into my arms!

Benjamin's party was a success, but what a zoo! Nine of the mothers I invited came to the party, bringing their one-year-olds as well as their other children. To feed the crowd, I made both egg-salad and tuna sandwiches, cutting them into quarters, in hopes they would stretch further. We also had carrot sticks, crackers and juice.

Realizing the two dozen chocolate cupcakes I had made were not going to reach, I was relieved when a few of the more "natural" moms refused the sugary treats for themselves and their kids.

Benjie, seated in his high-chair, camouflaged himself with chocolate cake and frosting after blowing out his single candle. There were spills and squabbles, balloons and wrappings, and ground-in cake crumbs everywhere, but everyone had a good time.

When I took Benjie down from his chair, he toddled away all by himself.

The next morning, when Jon gave me the grocery money, he also gave me the lowdown on more changes occurring in the house. He reported that Jay had found himself an apartment and wouldn't be returning. I was sorry to hear that; he would really be missed. Ted was again in the throes of a lengthy fast and had told Jon he wouldn't be eating at all this week. Pam was gone, having moved back home to her parents' before resuming dorm life at Portland State.

Alas, Dan had left for the mission field, giving his annoying dog to an unsuspecting family from church. Who knows? Maybe they would like the little beast.

And for some unknown reason, Gwen was returning on Monday to make dinner for us. Fine, I thought. At least that's one less meal I have to plan and buy. I wondered, though, was she trying to show me up or teach me a thing or two about ingenious new ways to feed this house? Was she intending to move in and take over my esteemed, though voluntary, position? Maybe I was over-thinking it and all she actually wanted to do was visit another house and share her "gift."

The previous Monday night, she had brought over a roaster of pre-made, ready to re-heat chicken-noodle-vegetable soup and a lovely loaf of whole wheat bread—all homemade and delicious, of course.

That evening it had become obvious some flirting was going on at the dinner table. Gwen must have had a crush on one of the brothers at Beth Israel and wanted to impress him with her cooking. Maybe it was the communal house equivalent of a date, I thought, secretly amused.

Being Apostolic Christian Church members, Don and I had never dated. Marriages are proposed solely on the basis of faith. After we became engaged, we were allowed to practice, instead, what some may refer to as "courtship." This meant we could only be together in the company of others, at church-related events or with him visiting my home in the presence of my parents and siblings.

But, hey—to borrow the most common clichés—I wasn't born yesterday and I certainly didn't live under a rock, thanks in part to Beth Israel. I could spot a date when I saw one.

I smiled to myself as I speculated on the idea of her coming over to a guy's house to cook dinner for him, but included in the deal were 14 additional mouths to feed and 28 more eyes gawking at her!

I hurriedly did my shopping that morning, and sped home in time to ready myself and my family for our professional portrait appointment. The studio was way out east, in Gresham, so it would take awhile to get there.

Our portrait plan, which we had nearly paid off, allowed for one 8x10 of each child and one 8x10 of the entire family, every year. We had Benjie's one-year-old picture taken that day, and the one of our family, but decided to wait until nearer Bethany's birthday, in December, to have hers done. Thankfully, June had dinner ready when we got home hot and tired, many hours later.

Monday afternoon, Gwen arrived earlier than I expected, carrying in two big, brown grocery bags. Keeping the contents of the bags a secret, she shooed me out of the kitchen saying, "I don't need your help with anything, except maybe to set the table. Don't put out plates, though. I'm preparing each person's meal individually and serving them myself." Wow, I thought, just like a restaurant. She's going to spoil these people for me.

When the time came and we were all seated hungrily at the foot of the *Last Supper* tapestry, Gwen brought out two brand-new bottles of store-bought salad dressing and set them lavishly on the table. This already smacked of luxury.

I always made our dressings "from scratch" in one of two predictable varieties: my "Ranch" was mayonnaise, sugar, oil and vinegar, and my "Thousand Island" was mayonnaise and ketchup with a sprinkling of utilitarian seasonings thrown in. I served the concoction in a worn Tupperware bowl with a plastic spoon stuck in it.

We all waited expectantly, stomachs growling, until finally the door swung open and she presented us with individual bowls of salad. I marveled at the amount of items on the salads. She had placed cherry tomatoes, black olives, sliced hard-boiled eggs and thin strips of ham and cheese on each. A separate bowl of crumbled bacon bits was passed around so that each person could crown their own masterpiece.

Everyone raved as the dressings were passed and house members doused their salads with extravagant amounts of the creamy condiment.

They all knew far too well what my salads looked like, little more than a torn head of lettuce with shredded carrot on top. Only occasionally could I spring for a tomato, or if I was lucky, someone from church would give us some from their garden.

"Wow! These salads are beautiful!" I complimented Gwen. "I can't make anything like this on our budget." I cast a glance at Jon, who turned his blushing face away. "You must have a lot more money to work with at your house than we do."

She watched as I took a bite, beaming proudly. "These are Chef Salads," she designated, nodding her head triumphantly.

"Yum!" said one of the impressed brothers before stuffing in another bite. "This is great! I can't wait to see what the main course is!"

Suddenly all color vanished from Gwen's face and she distinctly repeated, "These are Chef Salads." Then she forced a toothy smile and added, "They *are* the main course."

Forks paused in mid-air, the crescendo aborted. Gradually, everyone resumed eating in slow-motion, as the realization that this *was* dinner began to soak in. "Uh, well, they're real good salads," one brother offered, and others chimed in, attempting to endorse Gwen. For a few moments she looked caught in the quandary of whether to smile or cry.

And even though everyone exaggeratingly thanked her, she didn't return to make us dinner again. Any feelings of intimidation I had been harboring towards her were certainly gone now. I knew this salad-as-a-main-dish idea would never float at Beth Israel, not with this many brothers living here.

Not many days afterward, I discovered I was still wearing my sensitivity over meals and budgets on my shirtsleeves. At dinner one night, as we ate our meager ramen noodle soup, Tom raved about what great cooks his aunt and his grandmother were. Several other brothers joined him, sharing fond memories of huge feasts they had enjoyed at other homes.

Reaching my breaking point, I spouted off, "Anyone can be a good cook if they have lots of money to buy all the ingredients with! Don't you think we'd be eating like kings here if I had any money to work with? The trick is trying to be a good cook *without* it!"

I cleaned off my children's hands and faces, got them down from their chairs, and removed ourselves from the dining room. My attitude was racing down hill fast, and I didn't know how to stop it. Serving these people had become a dreadful chore and I was tired of it.

The house dynamics were changing once again, with summer winding down. Sue moved out and with her went the undisputed house favorite—cowboy coffee. I tried making it one more time after she left, but it just wasn't the same. She planned to attend a community college across the river.

Vanessa, though not technically *living* at Beth Israel, certainly returned for meals often enough. Gospel Outreach was pulling out of the communal houses, leaving town for their mission fields, so, sadly, we lost GO Don. There were noticeably fewer people at church, too.

I finally worked up the nerve to ask Don if we could discuss the possibility of our leaving Beth Israel. Intimidated by the steady diet of teachings on husbands and wives, and their authority and submission roles, I wasn't sure it was appropriate for me to suggest this. Maybe I should just pray about it privately and wait until he thinks of it himself, I tried to convince myself.

Many of the young couples and families who had always lived communally were leaving the houses and getting places of their own. We had begun with a place of our own and reverted to communal living, which seemed a little "out of sync."

"Why is it that we aren't supposed to *want* anything?" I stewed one evening, in the privacy of our room. "Is it actually a sin to want to have somewhere to call your own?"

We were consistently taught to live as though material things didn't matter. We were supposed to never hold on to anything and always be willing to let things go. But was this really necessary to godliness?

I divulged to Don an incident which I had recently heard about, as a case in point:

It involved a single sister in another of the communal houses who owned an antique piano. She was engaged to a brother from yet another house, and one day he was moving her piano from her parents' house to hers.

As he sped along Interstate-5, hauling the piano in the bed of a borrowed pick-up truck, he took an off-ramp a little bit too fast. The top-heavy upright somersaulted out of the truck, smashing into a million pieces on the concrete freeway exit. He lightly dismissed the loss with a typical Prince of Peace phrase, "It's all gonna burn, anyway."

Well, he sure got the burning part right. This sister exploded and, burning with anger, she broke their engagement and demanded that he return to the site and salvage the piano. His attempt was in vain, and their break-up was ugly.

God was beginning to make me aware that the "wind of His Spirit" is vital, even if it blows harshly. Because I realized we needed its movement and the growth it brings, I appreciated the lessons I was learning by living at Beth Israel—even though they were difficult and painful. But I just couldn't get my mind around the concept that valuing anything material made one a lesser person in God's eyes.

I came across a wonderful book titled *If I Can, You Can.* I had found it on the sale table—marked down to one dollar—at Christian Supply Center, when we stopped there briefly to browse on the way home from our photo appointment.

The author, Betty Estes, was married to a Messianic Jewish man whose life was always going "gang-busters." She told of honing her coping skills, handling crises, and also of sometimes "putting the brakes on" for her man when things got too frenzied. That was a new concept for me, for she was truly a godly woman, yet had a mind of her own and didn't just blindly submit to everything that came down the pike.

Her testimony strengthened and encouraged me, as I, too, was learning how to deal with people and situations while gaining victory over my fears and inhibitions.

I had learned to make a home for as many as 24 people and somehow embrace the chaos. I could keep things clean (if not spotless), practice hospitality without pretense, and reject the pressures I had previously borne — to always impress and perform. I had become much more tolerant, practical and somehow had even managed to maintain my sanity.

But something told me it was time to go.

Our family portrait— August, 1976

CHAPTER TWELVE

WINDS

By September we were down to the least number of people since our arrival; there were 10 adults and three children at Beth Israel. Those remaining were Jon, Ted, PSU-student Don, Tom, Kirk, Terry, Ann, June and her son, and our family.

When Jon handed me the grocery allotment that Saturday, a spartan $54, I knew I could never make it reach. Though we had fewer mouths to feed, we still had grocery staples and non-food supplies that needed to be maintained.

As Don handed our monthly bills over to Jon, he mentioned again that we had received late notices on our statements. This did no good, though. Why should we expect anyone else to take our finances as seriously as we did ourselves? This system just was *not* working. Not wanting to accrue late fees and a poor credit rating, we had to augment payments with what we could eke out of our allowance.

That Sunday, Chuck asked us if we could temporarily house a family of three. They were new to the church and the man had recently been laid off from his job. "It's cool," Don assured him. "We have plenty of room. We're down to a dozen people right now."

Chuck then brought us over to meet Bill, Diane and their son, a boy who looked to be about six. After introductions, we were left to visit with them and invited them to follow us home.

By playing a little housemate musical-chairs, no one ended up still standing without a room. When Jay moved out, he had vacated the small room off the dining room. It was now occupied by Tom, but he offered it to June, who in turn gave up her second-floor bedroom to the new family. Tom moved back into the basement.

After helping them get settled in, I explained the cooking and chores list to Diane, adding her name to the roll. She was more than willing to do her share but I found, in the coming days, that she was overly sensitive and I had to tip-toe cautiously around her.

Her husband, Bill, was to receive unemployment beginning the next week, but at present, they were broke. He was out looking for work a good portion of each day but, when he was home, they were often together behind the closed doors of their room.

I, uncomfortably, could hear them arguing and her crying. It became obvious that she didn't want to live in a communal house, missed her privacy and was ill at ease around so many strangers. Their son was to start first grade and she didn't know where to enroll him, as they had just moved from their rental house in the southeast district.

Feeling ashamed that they could not yet contribute financially, she offered to pay for and prepare a special dinner for the house on Thursday. She excitedly told me that, as a child, she had lived briefly in the "Far East," having missionary parents, and knew a great recipe for pork chow mein. Grateful for any relief to our menu and budget, I accepted her offer.

Returning from the grocery store that afternoon, she beamed with pride as she showed me her purchases and explained her intended method of preparation. I knew that she had spent their last remaining dollars. I watched as she placed a scant cut of pork roast into the oven to bake and then lovingly washed the snow peas and sliced the water chestnuts. She had a couple packages of Chinese noodles called "lo mein," which needed to be boiled.

Once again relegated from the kitchen, I merely set the table and waited for dinner like everyone else. I had told her to cook enough to serve at least 12, but as we were being seated, I noticed Vanessa was visiting again and Ted, apparently between fasts, surprised us with his presence. Now, including the new family, there were 16 hungry mouths to feed.

Diane proudly carried in her *piece de resistance* and set it down in front of Jon. He took a big helping and passed it on to Tom, who did likewise. "Can I help you bring in anything?" I asked innocently, noticing her pork dish was contained in an average-size serving bowl. I sure hoped she had padded it with a "side" or this meal was never going to reach.

She drew the same conclusion as she sat down, staring at the table full of people. "Oh, no! I didn't make enough," her voice broke. As the bowl passed from the third to fourth person, it was already half empty.

"Don't take so much, you guys," I warned, as Ted dug into the bowl.

"You should've told me there would be 16 here!" she accused, standing to her feet and looking directly at me. "This isn't even enough for six! Now I've ruined everyone's dinner." Weeping, she turned and ran from the table, climbed the stairs and slammed her door. Her husband was clearly embarrassed. He excused himself, rose from the table, took his son and followed her.

Everyone felt awkward and, not knowing what else to do, they scrambled to divvy up their portions with each other. I went to the kitchen to fetch some bread and butter, which always serves as filler in a pinch. It really did appear that she had made the recipe to serve six instead of 12. I wished she had noticed the sparse yield in time to throw together a salad or put out some bread to accompany it. If she had let me in the kitchen, I could have cooked up a saucepan of rice to mix in, thus doubling the yield. I hadn't realized until then how expert I had become at the art of improvisation.

We continued eating in silence, aware of her muffled, crying voice and his droning one overhead. Oh well, I thought, another one bites the dust. Bill and Diane weren't at Beth Israel long enough to donate that first unemployment check to the house.

The weather was turning cold already and Jon reinstated his decree that our gas furnace's thermostat be set no higher than 65 by day and 60 at night. However, during the day when Jon wasn't around, June took the liberty of raising the lever to 70. "It's freezing in here!" she declared. "I can't live like this and neither can my baby."

Well, I thought, so much for our well-instilled principles of "authority and submission." Her chutzpah was remarkable, especially since she may not have been contributing an income to the house. I liked being warm as much as the next person, but my husband's salary could only stretch so far.

One cloudy morning, about a week after Bill and Diane moved out, there was a rap at the door. I opened it and there stood Bill, with another man at his side, and an enormous six-foot-tall, refrigerator-size box on a dolly. A truck idled in the street, double parked.

Bill explained that he had been rehired at the grocery distribution warehouse where he had previously worked. They had an excess shipment of cereal that they were going to throw out, but he told them he knew of a place where it could be put to good use. "We have six cases of Cap'n Crunch "Punch Crunch" cereal in here," he laughed. "How much of it do you want?"

"Bring it all in," I smiled. "I'll make room for it." I wasn't about to turn away free food. Our pantry closet was nearly bare. I pushed things over and double stacked, easily emptying several shelves. I ran out of pantry space before emptying the first case of cereal, but the man with the dolly kept bringing in more. He began unloading them in the foyer since I couldn't keep up with him. After a moment of quick thinking, I constructed a ziggurat of boxes behind the kitchen nook door to finish emptying the first case.

"How about putting the other cases in the basement?" I suggested, and he did. If I had counted correctly, each case held forty-eight boxes of the red-berry flavored breakfast food, and we had six cases!

"Good-bye oatmeal and millet," I sang, after the men left. "Hello pink Punch Crunch!" I took my children's hands and we danced around the kitchen as I sang my little ditty. I was Miriam headily leading the Children of Israel in a song of praise when, after wandering for what seemed an eternity in the wilderness, God provided fresh "manna."

Caught up in the whirlwind of excitement, I seated the kids at the table and extravagantly poured each of us a bowl of the heavenly substance. We wolfed it down, confident there would be a fresh supply tomorrow.

As Don and the others arrived home that evening, I delightedly recounted the tale of our miraculous harvest. Over dinner we discussed how to fairly distribute the spoils. Doing some tallying, we determined that if each person were allotted one box of Punch Crunch each day, to do with as they wished, we would have almost enough to last us a month. Of course, it would be in lieu of any other breakfast cereal and all snacks. Now we only needed some additional milk and breakfast was covered for weeks!

After dinner clean-up, everyone filed into the kitchen and I passed out a box of cereal to each person. Each housemate immediately wrote his or her name on their box to avoid any mix-up.

Next morning at breakfast, everyone came to the table with their own box of Punch Crunch. Each person was free to eat it at their own discretion; some chose to eat more at breakfast, finishing it as an evening snack, and others did the opposite.

We all enjoyed a good laugh as we imagined the fit Monica would have if she were living here now. We were indulging ourselves in the two deadliest of sins, in her mind—processed white sugar and red food dye!

A few days into the diet, I noticed my kids' poops were now a deep maroon. I was amused to imagine that this was plaguing the other housemates as well. Nevertheless, each morning the sister on breakfast duty simply put out a new box of Punch Crunch at each place setting, and then had extra time to join everyone in the parlor prayer meeting.

One September day, completely out of the blue, Jon mentioned to Don that he was curious about the Rosh Hashanah service at our neighborhood synagogue. He asked Don if he would be interested in checking it out with him.

Don jumped at the chance to experience a Jewish New Year rite, and asked if I could go as well. But Jon informed us that the Orthodox congregation was for men only.

Temple Beth Israel was a stately, golden-domed, stone edifice that we had often passed when taking walks. Jon and Don walked there together and sat in the balcony and tried to remain inconspicuous, despite the fact that they were the only men not wearing the traditional "kippots" on their heads.

Don was fascinated by the Hebrew prayers, songs and readings and developed an instant partiality to his own Jewish roots. His great-grandfather, August "Kramer," was a Dutch Jew who had married a Roman Catholic, French-Canadian woman. At her insistence, they had changed the spelling of their surname to the French rendering "Cremer." No reference to their Jewish-ness was ever made in his grandfather's household, due to the unpopularity of such a stigma in the early twentieth-century. By the time Don's generation rolled around, it was completely forgotten. But attending this Rosh Hashanah service sparked a predisposition in him that has continued to burn to this day.

On their walk home, Don snatched the opportunity to discuss some house issues with Jon. He pointed out that the 100% system was not equitable for us, as our bills were still being neglected and the needs of our family were not being met. Working up his nerve, he took a deep breath and told Jon he could no longer sign his paychecks over to the house, adding that we were considering moving out soon.

Jon seemed so okay with this information that Don wondered why he hadn't spoken up sooner. Jon confided to him that, even though the 100% system was officially in effect, he was allowing some people to pay rent, and if we returned to paying rent it would be fine. On a roll, he also disclosed to Don that he himself had considered leaving Beth Israel soon, and maybe even moving to Europe.

Later, as Don relayed their conversation to me, for some reason, I was shocked. But slowly we began to realize that, when it came right down to it, everyone really *could* choose to live their own lives.

Here, this person we had been so intimidated by turned out to be just a regular guy.

Out of ear-shot, Don ruminated, "Why is it that some people refuse to submit to a system, do whatever they want and they get away with it? Yet we obey all the rules, submit to whatever group we're with, do everything just right, and we end up getting screwed?"

Don and I had gone directly from one set of restrictions, in the Apostolic Christian Church, to another in the Prince of Peace. The scripture warns against always being blown around by "every wind of doctrine." Maybe it was about time for us to begin discovering a moderate stance of our own.

We talked about how the "weaving together"—like it said on a bookmark I had—of such varied personalities produces a ragged texture. We tend to see only the underside, with all its knots and snags. God sees the top of the perfected tapestry and, every now and then, He grants us a glimpse at the glory, lest we get discouraged.

Though Don admitted he would have been satisfied to stay on at Beth Israel indefinitely, he recognized my need for us to be a private family again. I was relieved that God had intervened, granting us an opportunity to finally discuss it. Because of my indoctrination, I would have felt guilty purloining a pinch of privacy from my husband.

Over the weekend, we began scouring the classified ads, looking for a house or apartment to rent. Prices had gone up during our stay at Beth Israel. We made lots of calls and did some looking, while remaining hush-hush. We didn't want the housemates to know yet, just in case it didn't work out.

On Monday morning, a chilly wind was blowing as I saw Don off to work. I felt hopeless and distraught at the prospect of facing another week of the stress-filled life at the house. I struggled deeply with my desires to have our own privacy and independence again, still viewing it as a spiritual issue.

Aware that a storm was gathering, I knelt to pray at the red leather chair in our room, watching the sky blacken. When the clouds suddenly capitulated and a heavy rain splattered against the panes, my tears simultaneously began to fall. I prayed, earnestly pouring out my heart to God and the storm answered, raging with thunder and lightning.

At length, with both the clouds and my tear ducts emptied, I lifted my head and looked out the north-facing window at the soggy neighborhood. There, to my amazement, was the closest and most vivid rainbow I had ever seen. I reached towards it like a child, half expecting that I could touch it if I opened my window. I stared in awe at the brightness of the colors and marveled that I could view the complete bow, both ends touching down on the newly-washed world.

God reminded me of His Genesis promise to Noah—in the sign of the rainbow—that He would not destroy His own, but would propagate them in a restored land. Thanking God for His assurance, I got up off the floor and sat in the chair letting my Bible fall open on my lap.

My gaze fell on Psalm 84 and I read, "Passing through the valley of weeping, He makes it a place of springs." This beautiful promise wrought my healing. I sprang to my feet, twirled around and lifted my arms in praise, elevated anew by the ethers of possibility!

The changing season brought a new brother to Beth Israel. He took one look at the overgrown jungle of weeds in the backyard and declared that something must be done about it. He recruited the single guys to join him in forming a work-force for that next Saturday morning.

They worked for hours clearing the growth, hauling away most of it and mulching down what remained. He then ordered several cords of wood to be delivered, and the guys stacked the logs neatly in the tidy backyard. When they were finished, it was unrecognizable.

Here, all it took was for someone to identify the need and do something about it. I was in awe of God again, accepting how He places people where He wants them and distributes "giftings" according to need. Now there was plenty of wood to burn in the fireplace this winter and a turned over garden plot in case someone wanted to plant next spring.

The last Saturday night of September, Don went out preaching from the Prince of Peace Coffeehouse with Nick. Don had not mentioned that we were looking for a place to move, but Nick began telling him how he and his wife had just become apartment managers at a large complex in Oregon City. It was a decent place in a more rural location out of the city, and the best part was the rent was pro-rated according to one's income. Don asked him if there was anything available on the first of the month, so Nick said he would check on it and give us a call.

A couple days later Nick telephoned us and reported, "There are currently no openings, but I'll put you on the list if you want. Maybe something will come up for the fifteenth."

Shortly after that, still without our telling anyone of our intentions, a single sister from another house expressed interest in moving into Beth Israel, with the eventual goal of becoming a kitchen steward. She moved in that weekend and proved to be a real boon to the house, level-headed and ambitious. All she wanted from life was to serve and I assured her she would fulfill her wish at Beth Israel.

On October 7th, Nick called to say an apartment was available on the 15th. It was a three bedroom, two-story townhouse, right across the courtyard from theirs. Sight unseen, we agreed to take it and arranged to drive down there on Saturday to see it.

Come Saturday morning, we set out on the thirty-five minute drive, heading south through Portland's west side and then crossing the Sellwood Bridge, near where I lived as a child. We continued south on Highway 99E, through the suburbs. Once we got to Oregon City, we climbed the three hills and headed out of town towards Molalla.

The clouds were exceptional that morning. They were completely flat at the bottom—as if they had been piled onto God's table, then rose in voluminous billows, with golden rays spreading out from behind like bicycle spokes. I received it as a special sign from Him; He was spreading a table of blessing before us and we were preparing to partake.

We loved the apartment and its roomy layout. The living room, combination dining and family room, storage closet and kitchen were on the first floor. Three bedrooms, the bathroom and another large storage closet were on the second. There was ample yard and even a playground for the kids.

Don produced his most recent paycheck stubs and Nick's wife tallied up our rent—one-fourth of our gross monthly income. Our rent, with Don's recent raise, would be $160 per month. We had deposited a paycheck of Don's into our bank account for the first time in six months, thus saying good-bye to the 100% system. He wrote the check for our first month's rent and set our moving date for the following Saturday, October 16th, my birthday.

On the drive home, we discussed how Jesus had said, in John 3:8, something to the effect that "The wind blows wherever it wants, and since you can't see it, you never know which way it's coming from or where it's going next. You can, however, see the *effects* of the wind. So it is," He had concluded, "in the lives of those who are led by the Spirit." It became one of our favorite verses, for now we could relate to it in real life.

At dinner we announced that we were planning to move out the following weekend. Everyone expressed sadness to see us go. "You guys are so good at this," June piped up. "Don't you think you'd want to be "house heads" again?"

I surprised myself by answering with an insight I had not possessed before Beth Israel. "It's not that we wouldn't be open to it, but I don't think we'll find our way back into serving God in exactly the same way again. God has so much variety that He rarely replicates an experience. I think He works according to the necessity of the moment."

During the coming week, I re-gathered our personal belongings from the far corners of the house. The majority of our things were still stacked where we had left them, in the attic, although it appeared the attic-dwellers had been helping themselves to the use of our linens, pillows and lamps. Pulling out my kitchenware from the drawers and cupboards left quite a void, so I ended up donating several items that seemed essential to the house.

We also decided to leave a few of our books and Bibles in the parlor bookcase and a wooden plaque that read "For God hath not given us the spirit of fear; but of power, and of love, and of a sound mind. - II Timothy 1:7"

On Thursday, June prepared a nice dinner for the house and surprised me with a store-bought cake. All the housemates had signed a card for me and sang *Happy Birthday* around the table. I was so touched that I cried, realizing it was also good-bye.

Following dinner, Don removed our *Last Supper* tapestry from the wall, for it was our last supper at Beth Israel. The bare wall above the wainscoting portrayed the empty hole we would be leaving by our departure.

To make use of our built-in babysitters one last time, Don surprised me with his plan to take me to The River Queen restaurant for a birthday dinner, on Friday night. It was pricey, but we still had a little money stashed away from our weekly allowances. We had never been there before, but Don managed to maneuver through downtown and found it, impressively docked on the Willamette River.

He knew how much I loved anything having to do with the Civil War and steamboat era, and this was probably the closest I would ever come. We ordered mint juleps—something I had only fantasized about in my reading of Southern historical novels—and imagined we were floating down the Mississippi delta.

Over dinner, Don told me that he had, just that morning, met the new "yuppie" couple who recently moved into the house next door. They were headed down their stoop towards their respective cars, both in business attire—he in a suit and tie and she in a dark skirt, cowl-neck sweater and blazer.

During their brief exchange, Don learned that they both worked downtown and had bought the old house to renovate and re-sell it. Previously, the house had been rented by a reclusive hippie couple. Don told the new couple that we would be moving out the next day, and that he was sorry we wouldn't get to know them.

Bittersweet emotions flooded me as I gazed out the window watching the wind raise little white-caps on the ruffling river. Perhaps in this passing, we were witnessing the end of an era—not just in our personal lives, but in all of American society; the ushering in of a whole new way of life.

EPILOGUE

We made our exodus from Beth Israel on my 22nd birthday. As expected, it was another windy, overcast day as we transported our lives and belongings to yet another location. We made a couple of trips using Nick's pick-up truck, and a few Beth Israelites drove down separately, helping us move our boxes and smaller items into the apartment.

Later that afternoon as I was laying shelf paper in the kitchen cupboards, June came looking for me saying, "There's a delivery for you." I thought she must be kidding, because the door was constantly in motion as people continued carrying in our furnishings. I followed her to the front door and found a young man from a floral shop standing there.

"Judy Cremer?" he confirmed, checking the card.

"Yes," I answered.

"Then this is for you," he smiled, handing me a potted plant arrangement.

"Thank you," I extended my hands to receive it, delighted, but puzzled over who would have sent it to me.

Taking the green glazed planter, I walked over to the couch and sat down, admiring the three variegated plants it held. A large red bow was tied around it and a decorative butterfly pick stood in the soil. Cradling it on my lap, I opened the card. It was from my parents! The card read "Happy Birthday and Happy Moving Day, dear Judy! - Love, Mom and Dad." Sentiment and nostalgia swept over me, and I began to weep.

I had called to give them our new address a few days earlier and my mom had not forgotten me. I shouldn't have been surprised, but I was, because my life seemed so far away and far removed from hers.

I wondered if, when she ordered this arrangement today, she had remembered another move that was made on my birthday—my third one— in 1957. One of my earliest memories is of being bedded down for a nap with a satiny, rose-colored comforter on the hardwood floor in an empty room of our new house.

Don continued working at Reed Electric only briefly after our move. His preaching mentor, Ron, hatched plans to return to the University of California at Berkeley in November, to retrieve the degree he had earned from studying there years earlier. Ron asked Don, Nick and a couple other preaching buddies to accompany him, thus turning it into a week-long, outreach trip to the San Francisco Bay Area. Don gave notice at his job, as he didn't plan to return to it when he got back.

Don and his comrades traveled by van, spending their nights at Lighthouse Ranch and other Gospel Outreach enclaves. Following in the footsteps of the beleaguered Berkeley street-preaching icon, Holy Hubert, Don's adventures included being handcuffed and thrown into a squad car for preaching near a porno shop in the notorious Castro District.

I seized this opportunity to make a pilgrimage of my own and decided to take the kids down to visit my family in southern California. I made the unsuitable decision to go by Greyhound, which turned into an opportunity to test-drive my new wedding ring.

When our bus inappropriately stopped at a honky-tonk in California's Central Valley, a cowboy sauntered over and asked me to join him for a drink and a dance. Flashing him my left hand, I found that a little wedding band goes a long way. I couldn't help but laugh at how desperate he must have been to hit on someone with two toddlers in tow.

Upon returning to our new digs in Oregon City, Don partnered with Nick and started up a vinyl and leather-repair business they called "Good News." We managed to save a little money each month towards a down-payment, and somehow bought our first home less than a year later.

Our involvement with the Prince of Peace Fellowship continued until 1982. During these years, we experienced life on the cutting edge of a church, a movement and a generation; our most intense period unmistakably being the ten months we lived at Beth Israel. Never in the 30 years since then have we encountered so much of life compacted into such a small time-frame. To this day, we count our Beth Israel days as our most formative, our Beth Israel memories as our most vivid.

Why is that, we wonder? Was it our age, our time of life? Or was it the times in which we lived? The emphasis of the POP teachings was on facing our fears and walking through, rather than running from, them. We were taught to pray first in every situation, then follow the Holy Spirit, rather than relying on the "world's" way of solving crises.

We entered Beth Israel virginal in so many ways and emerged well-seasoned. Truly a watershed experience for us, it birthed the arduous process of changing us from restricted, legalistic Christians into emerging, global ones. I only regret that we were not able to give more to the community, rather than needing so often to be receivers, but we ourselves were constantly teetering on the brink of indigence. Even so, we were used by God as a channel for His provision.

"All my changes were there…," muses Neil Young, while pondering a formative place in his past, in his song *Helpless*. We echo this sentiment in referring to our Beth Israel days, for when we are most helpless and vulnerable, we are open and susceptible to the most change. Religion, which literally means "re-alignment or re-connectedness with God," is born of our vulnerability, as well as the moments He grants us brief divine insight. As we abandoned our fears and inhibitions, we gained an indelible print of God on our lives.

Only with age have I come to realize how much we and our contemporaries agonized over our search for "God's will." This over-thinking, over-exaggerating and over-dramatizing the finding and implementing of God's will was the burning motivation behind every quest we allowed, every decision we made.

Admittedly, this illusive component led us into some wild pursuits. But, as Ralph Waldo Emerson observed, "Nothing great is ever achieved without enthusiasm." Interestingly, the root word for enthusiasm is *entheos*, meaning "full of God."

I am finally beginning to understand that fulfilling God's will depends on trusting God's ways, then embracing Him and what He's doing *wherever* you find yourself. God's will is being achieved in whatever we are doing if we love Him. He comes to us as a gift, not as a result of our works or rules. For honestly, what can we render to God?

"Hey, this story ain't no tale to me now, for the Prince of Peace has given me life, somehow. You know what I mean...," sings *2ⁿᵈ Chapter of Acts* in *The Prince Song.*

And for us, that carries double significance.

Printed in the United States
77929LV00004B/262-492